How to Open your Own

In-Home Bookkeeping Service

I.S.B.N. 13   978-0-9746093-9-3

I.S.B.N. 9   0-9746093-9-0

Perfect Bound Publication

Replaces Spiral Bound Publication - ISBN 978-0-9746093-3-1

Author: Julie A. Mucha-Aydlott, CFE

Published by: San Diego Business Accounting Solutions, Inc. a "Non" CPA Firm

P.O. Box 1128

Lakeside, CA 92040

Printed in the United States

Graphic Design: Urick Designs   www.urickdesign.com

Author's Note: For those of you who notice a typo or grammatical error here and there, my apologies. I'm only human. Each publication does go back through an editing process, and I cannot guarantee that all misspelled words are caught. Not even my Fraud Legal Library is free from an occasional typo. Some excerpts and chapters from this book are pulled from the original book "How to Open Your Own In-Home Bookkeeping Service." Both books are published and written by Julie A. Mucha-Aydlott.

Dedication

To my Mom Beverly Mucha, who has paved the way for me
with her strength, ambition and giving heart. An incredible
woman who has taught me so much! I admire her more than she could
possibly know. Every day I pray for the strength to help
me through this tough time, and every day I am grateful to have been
blessed to have such a wonderful mother as you!
Not a day will pass by that I haven't thought of you many times.

About the Author

Excerpt portions from *"I have QuickBooks, Now What"* © 2005

In 1994 I opened my own accounting service because I, like many other aspiring individuals, cannot work for someone else. I work well with others, but require the respect and freedom that self-employment brings. With over fourteen years of accounting experience, I have gained the respect and drive that I have searched for. I am not going to write this bio in the third person. I am writing this to you as if I were sitting in your office teaching you my secrets of opening and running a successful bookkeeping and accounting service. I am not your typical accountant. I don't believe in the intimidation factor. Just because you have a title that deals with numbers and money, doesn't mean that you need to confuse or intimidate your clients. I do claim to be an expert in my field of discussion because I have set up, cleaned up, and made into perfection my clients' wishes with their books. I am an entrepreneur of sorts, and between writing these books, servicing my clients and raising my girls, I have changed a good portion of the accounting that I offer. I have always been a more analytical accountant instead of being so systematic that it's no longer fun. "Fun" – what kind of a sick person would even think accounting is fun? You do, because you're buying this book! I am much more self-rewarded with investigating financial crimes, so I have chosen to complete my studies to become a C.F.E. (Certified Fraud Examiner). In the meantime, here is my brain in the form of an updated version of the first book which I was very proud to have so many people find useful! My complete best wishes to you and your success.

Julie A. Aydlott

Table of Contents

Introduction

If your interest is to open an In-Home Bookkeeping or Accounting Service, your decision to purchase this book may be one of the smartest moves you've ever made! This book holds the past ten years of my mistakes, successes and stresses. It's easier for me to say this because I'm sitting at the other end of the computer writing this to you, but the only honest hardworking approach that you're going to get is by getting inside someone else's head to see what they've been through. I have recently just celebrated 10 years in business. That means that I have not had to ask someone else's permission to go home sick, pick up my children or beg for a vacation. I guarantee you this, though; it is hard work! Nothing comes easy, and I'm not going to tell you that it's a cakewalk. You have to dedicate yourself to your success; otherwise the next person who purchased this book from me is going to beat you to the punch. I decided to write a second edition to the original book with a few things in mind. I get an incredible feeling of accomplishment when so many of you have purchased my books send me updates and emails to let me know how you're doing and how much the books have helped. I know I can add updates and additional information that I have learned along the way, as I have asked many of you for your unanswered questions. This book is going to have additional items on services and marketing. The biggest question that you ask me is, "What do I say to get a client?" There will be a lot of the same chapters in this book as the first one – no need to re-invent the wheel! For those of you who are just tuning into me, and my personality, I tend to be on the honest, fun side, so if my humor comes out, sorry, I can't help it. I guess that is what makes me different than the next guy. You don't need to be uptight and impersonable. This world is too short, and I intend to live it my way; just remember, you only get one life, so make it a good one. Most of you who searched the Internet to find me have also found other businesses out there that tell you you're going to make millions instantly, and the fine print has a hefty price tag attached to it. There are a few websites out there that offer advice on opening your own bookkeeping service. My books have been around for over five years, and I'm not going through a publishing house that likes to exclude reality. So everything that you read within these pages is as truthful as it's going to get. I was just like you in 1994. I was scared to death. I knew I couldn't work for anyone. I hated being labeled and not in control of my life. Not everyone can be self-employed. It takes a rare, dedicated individual with ambition and guts to take the leap of faith and just do it. A good number of us didn't quit our day job until we had enough to make it to the other side. But then guess what, when it's 3:15 in the afternoon, being a need-exercise-to-relieve-stress kinda gal, I am going to go running because I can. I can write myself into my calendar; I make myself an appointment at 3:15 to run 2 ½ miles to relieve my tension buildup. How many can say they have the ability to add themselves to their list of duties without being told "no." I am not a motivational speaker, but I do hope to open your eyes to your goals. No one can reach them but you. If I can give a little push, then my job is done.

In this book, you will learn the necessary tools and information to open and successfully operate your own bookkeeping service. If you are starting your bookkeeping business without any knowledge in the accounting or bookkeeping industry, you will need additional educational resources. This book is geared towards individuals who have a basic understanding of bookkeeping, and was written with the "How did you do it?" questions in mind. There are many great educational resources to enhance your knowledge and service ability. This book is written to guide you in what you need to do as a bookkeeping service. I have included the Certification Application from the American Institute of Professional Bookkeepers along with their contact information, plus contact and class information for an online accounting school. If you are not confident with your bookkeeping skills, the AIPB (American Institute) website has a free bookkeeping test. Take the test, see where your skills are weak, and focus on that area.

With this book, you will learn how to set up accounting books, starting with your own. You will become much more effective with your work habits, and will build a confidence that you never knew you had! I don't know how many times I got butterflies in my stomach at a job interview – not knowing if I said the right thing to get the job, and knowing that I always had to get backed into a corner from a boss who was on an authority trip. When you work for yourself, you represent yourself, and when you walk into a potential client's office, you are not afraid of an "interview"; you are the interview, because it is your future and goals that you are striving for. You show the client what they need in their accounting department to more effectively and efficiently run their business. Your confidence and self-esteem can grow so high! No more sitting at work wondering what it would be like to be your own boss! You have taken the first step to make valuable and important decisions about your future, rather than having someone decide them for you! You can decide when to make your appointments, and go to that Christmas play that your child is in without feeling guilty from having a boss who doesn't agree with families coming first!

I have developed my skills and experience over the past 14 years, which has made me and my business who I am today. Most associates and clients find my down-to-earth approach easier to understand and they feel more comfortable with it. Some people have not. I have found that the ones who have not are the ones who can't look outside the box and don't like someone like me who is carefree to change the rules. I have changed the rules because I can; and you, the ones buying my books, appreciate the matter-of-fact honesty that you're looking for. I'm not an infomercial that promises instant millions, nor a politically correct author who writes what I'm told by making it "stay in the box." You want to know! I'm opening you up to my brain without covering up the important questions, the ones that no one else likes to answer. I must be doing something right . . . 10 years later and I'm still not punching someone else's time clock!

Gather your ideas and thoughts, and have a nice pad of paper handy because you need to record what is happening in your brain as you begin to read this book and get your own ideas.

Chapter 1
Where to begin

A successful business owner always learns from their mistakes! Everyone makes them, and I'm going to show you how to avoid them. Make sure you take notes and mark off the items you complete!

- ✓ Select a name for your new company. If you choose a name associated with your own name, whether it is your first or last, you will <u>not</u> have to pay additional charges for filing a "Fictitious Business Name."

- ✓ If you select a company name such as "A-1 Bookkeeping," you will have to go to the city you're located in and file a fictitious business application. Along with the application fee, usually around $25 depending on the city you live in, you need to publish that name in a local newspaper as well. A fictitious name is usually good for 5 years; check with your city government office. It should say how long it's active for on the application. You will normally get a renewal notice in the mail when it's time to renew. If you do not renew the name and you are using an expired name, someone else can come along and use your company's name. It is like incorporating. The state requires you to do a search for the name that you wish to use to make sure no one else is already using that name. If you end up using someone else's company name and they find out, you can be sued. Normally it would just turn into a Cease and Desist order: a "Quit using it or else" threat.

- ✓ Apply for your City Business License. You must have this to operate your business out of your home. A City License usually costs $25 and will renew every year on your anniversary date. Contact your local city government office to get an application for your business. (If you rent your house, you <u>must</u> get permission from your landlord to operate a business out of the home; you need to do this to keep everything legal). Have your landlord sign a letter stating that they are aware that you are operating a business in their home, and that they agree with it. Some local city offices may not require you to obtain permission to operate a business out of your home even if it's rented, but this day and age when people are so sue-happy, it might be in your best interest to do it anyway just for your protection.

✓ Once you receive your business license, you can open a checking account at your local bank. Since you are just starting your business, select an account with low activity and no monthly service fee. They do have programs available. When your activity increases, they would be happy to switch your account program to suit your business. Instead of paying over $50 for checks from your bank in that nifty little checkbook, remember you are going computerized! Pass on the checks from the bank and order computerized checks. You can order 500 computerized QuickBooks or Peachtree checks from a company called Checkfamous. Their website address is www.checkfamous.com. Even Intuit® can't beat their price of $49.95! **Build a relationship with your bank, especially the "New Accounts" manager.**

✓ Learn how to set up your own accounting software! The best place to start is with your own business. There are two software programs that I recommend. Most of your clients will request or already use QuickBooks Pro® because of the ease of understanding the software. If you go with the lowest-end version of QuickBooks, it's still very basic bookkeeping. Their software has become much more complex for the <u>client</u> so it is more work for you the bookkeeper to train the client on all of its functions. This brings you back to the client to keep billing them, but also can frustrate the client because of lack of understanding.

- The most widely used software of course is **QuickBooks Pro®**. The majority of the CPA firms use this program because it is easy for their clients to operate. Learn the program inside and out! I guarantee you will be approached by clients to train employees on how to successfully use the software as well as "setting up" your clients' software and complete accounting system. **QuickBooks Pro®** is around $199.95, but before you buy the software you need to understand the difference between that and the version of software you need to use for your clients. Order and install the Trial Software from Intuit's QuickBooks Pro® website at

www.quickbookspro.com. You have 15 uses on this disk. After you are comfortable with the software, and have set up your company's accounting, I suggest that you apply to become a QuickBooks Pro Advisor. The software will be included in the dues for becoming a professional advisor, and you will get all of the benefits of being a Pro-Advisor, like client referrals. You can sign up online at: **http://www.intuitadvisor.com/expand_practice/qb_advisor/index.html**

- Or call their toll-free number located in the important contacts in the back of this book. Quicken® Turbo Tax® and QuickBooks® are a registered trademark of Intuit®.

- If you order the full software online, it would benefit you more if you signed up for the Pro-advisor program with QuickBooks Pro®. It costs around $299.95 to sign up and take the test. It provides you with discounted rates on your software for your clients, along with putting your name on their website's contact distributor list. You can also become a Certified Pro-Advisor. This test costs around $529.95, which includes the software, and placement at the top of their website contact pro-advisor lists, plus you get to use their trademark name for a Certified Advisor.

- What version of QuickBooks® is important for your service? In the services lesson I will be more detailed on what the software can do for you and your clients, but for now, it is important that you know what type of service you want to provide. If you are going to "service" your clients at their office, then the less expensive version of QuickBooks Pro® would be adequate for your needs at your own office. If you will be working via remote access, which is the best timesaving tool because of commuting, there are two options that you must use. QuickBooks Pro® has gotten much more expensive because of the possibilities with the software. It is worth the extra money for the convenience. The software is growing with the client's needs rather then the client outgrowing the software within a few years. For remote access, you will need the Premier Accountant Version of QuickBooks Pro®, for $379.95. This edition is not network ready, but Intuit® is working on it as we speak. Your client will need the Premier Edition costing $379.95 for one user; but this version is network capable with up to 5 users simultaneously on the computer at one time for $799.95. If they were already a QuickBooks Pro® user, the upgrade is $649.95. As a Pro-Advisor, you can get the software for your clients at up to 20% of suggested retail price. Remember though, when you become a Pro-Advisor, the Premier Accountant version of software is included in your advisor package.

- A second choice of software is Peachtree®. In times past, Peachtree® used to be more integrated for the CPA and Accountant than for the client. It was difficult to understand and to use unless you understood accounting. They have upgraded the software to become more compatible with the end user. It is much easier to use and to understand. If you have clients that book inventory and are in the manufacturing or retail business, Peachtree® will be the best software to use, hands down. The inventory portion of their program is above all the others in keeping consistent and accurate inventory values and totals. I also really appreciate the way Peachtree® will close out the accounting month and force you to switch months before you can change any prior data. That is very important especially if you have clients using the software who like to go back and change things, e.g., making your Year-End Balance Sheet no longer equal the Corporate Tax Returns Balance Sheet. However, Peachtree® has not yet enabled you to import your journal entries and changes to your clients via disks, so you would have to do all your work at your client's office, which isn't a bad thing.

  - Peachtree's® costs are very similar to QuickBooks Pro®. The regular complete accounting version is $299.95, the multi-user version is $699.95, and the lower-end accounting version is $199.95.

  - You can also become a Peachtree Advisor. The membership fee is $100, and is an annual membership. You sign up with the Best

Software Accountants Network which enables you not to just limit yourself to only one software; they also train on Timeslips, MAS90, MIP and many more. The Peachtree complete Library costs around $295 to sign up, then $195 per year after that. Which brings your total Peachtree Advisor costs to around $395 as your initial signup costs. They supply the 5-User version of software, customer support, and tax tables. It's a very good price for what they supply, considering their software also starts at $299.95. Peachtree is marketing their accountant programs pretty diligently right now, so they are offering discounts on memberships to try and get QuickBooks® advisors going to their side as well. I have enclosed their enrollment form for your convenience. You can also download it, for use with Adobe Acrobat Reader, from www.bestaccountantsnetwork.com. Peachtree's® contact and website information is located at the back of this book with your other important phone numbers.

- My advice and suggestion is to initially concentrate on just one software while you are starting your business. However, order the Peachtree Trial Software as well and install it so you can learn both of them. You will be more valuable knowing more than one software, and you will get business for that knowledge. Most of the small business world knows and requests QuickBooks Pro® because it is more widely known and used. Use Peachtree as a back-up resource for knowledge and clients who keep inventory. Either way, you're going to be the one suggesting which software you prefer and which would be best suited for the client. What a wonderful thing, to have someone actually care about your opinion and suggestion. Respect isn't easy to come by, but you earn it when you work for yourself!

✓ Business Cards and Letterhead! An office supply store is a great place to go to find programs to create your own business cards and letterhead. If it's not in your budget to go to a printer, get creative and do it yourself! They carry so many different types of background paper to create your own business cards; in the beginning operation it will save you a lot more money to do it yourself. However, you can find a small print shop, even Office Depot® or your local office supply store, and it will be more cost-effective to print your business cards and letterhead in a larger quantity. Kinko's will give you pretty good deals on printing if you are a consistent and polite customer. There is one Kinko's assistant manager, Norbert, who has saved the day for me many of times, even if they are doing a small job. I never understood why he was just the assistant manager. With the service he provides to his client base, who ask for him by name, for some reason when the manager of the store went to a different Kinko's they didn't give him the promotion, so he followed the other manager. He still takes care of me being another 25 miles away! If you are just running small jobs, even if they are postcards, brochures, letterheads and business cards, they can give you a good deal. Just find the right sales associate and ask.

✓ Create a budget for your company. Document your ideas, what you need to begin, and see where your personal finances allow you to proceed. I have included a "general budget" on what your expected beginning capital requirements are to open a bookkeeping service. It is not that costly. You would be surprised how much equipment you already have to begin your company.

✓ Organize your office to meet your needs. Make sure you can find all of your notes, forms, and documentation. If you organize yourself first, you'll be much more prepared to organize your clients.

✓ Get a second phone line in your house. You <u>don't</u> want your clients to have your home number. I guarantee they will call you evenings, weekends and holidays. If you can afford it, get voice mail hookup from your local phone company. It is a lot better than an answering machine because if someone calls and you're on the other line, it will go into voice mail and you'll never lose a message. Not that we don't appreciate our clients, but you have a personal life too, and clients who think they're having an emergency at 8:30 at night might not be considerate of our personal life.

✓ As soon as you're comfortable setting up your own software (whether it's QuickBooks® or Peachtree®) and feel you are familiar with the program, and your business license is up and running, you can start your contacts. **Do not start until you feel ready.**

✓ Start talking to friends, family members, old contacts, etc., and let them know you started up "A-1 Bookkeeping Service." Begin getting the word out.

✓ Miscellaneous items that you will need to organize your home office:

- o Filing cabinet
- o Hanging file folders
- o General office supplies
- o Address stamp pad or labels
- o Three-ring binders with monthly dividers
- o Ten Key
- o P.O. Box (when soliciting, you don't want your home address given out to anyone). Women! Be very careful about who you give out your home address to! Even though we are just as capable and equal to run a business, we aren't as physically strong as men because their bodies are built for endurance, ours are built for childbirth. It takes one bad choice and the person we thought was a new client coming over could be a criminal rapist.
- o GBC 100E Velobinder with report covers. The machine is about $99 at an office supply store and the report covers are around $14.99 for 25. The plastic combs are around $10.99 for a box of 25. It looks so much more professional than the binders that I used to give to my clients. (This machine is not mandatory.)
- o Get a day-timer, even if it is a notepad! You need to keep track of your appointments, and your "Things to do" list. It is also a diary that holds more tax verification than you could possibly know! If you ever had to prove or disprove a theory to the IRS regarding whether or not you took Suzie from Paychex to lunch on March 7th at 1:00, if it was written in your daytimer, you now have evidence to back up your receipt if ever questioned!

It is time to begin your lessons! Take notes, and <u>always</u> write down your ideas. Even if they seem irrelevant at the time, they could be a great tool later!

Starting with your own books

The first place to start is with your own books! This will give you the best insight to what you are about to create for other companies. Whether or not you have opened a business checking account, or you are using your personal checking account to start up your company, you still need to keep track of your expenses if you want to write them off at the end of the year.

Start with your expenses. Keep a running expense log handy for all the costs you encounter setting up your company – whether it is for gasoline, this instruction book, computer software or business cards.

Your general startup expenses will be from your personal cash, checking, or credit cards. Keep good records! You are not only doing this for yourself, but for other companies. They always say a mechanic drives a junky car, so <u>don't</u> ever fall into that category!

Go through the tutorial if you don't know QuickBooks® or Peachtree. They will both take you through a step-by-step tutorial on how to set up a new company. The best thing about QuickBooks Pro® is that you can set up a multitude of companies. You aren't excluded to only one. I suggest if you have never used Quicken® Microsoft Money, or something similar like that, take the tutorial in QuickBooks® to show you the functions of the software. It will help you to learn the program; however, if you need help understanding QuickBooks® and want the best layman's way of setting up companies as well as understanding bookkeeping, my other book, **"I Have QuickBooks, NOW WHAT?"** (formerly *Computerized Bookkeeping in Laymen's Terms©*), will open your eyes to many misunderstood questions and will be the easiest and quickest resource on setting up QuickBooks®. QuickBooks® was designed for <u>non-accountants</u>. It really does all of the work for you. Peachtree® has been redeveloped so the business owner and bookkeeper could use its powerful tools. However, as a bookkeeper or accountant, you will double-check the entries and work.

Keep in mind that this book does not teach you QuickBooks Pro® or Peachtree® step by step; rather it teaches you step by step what a bookkeeping service provides.

You are a service company. Set up your chart of accounts accordingly. It has been my experience, especially because I have created my own numbering format for my chart of accounts, to modify the accounts that QuickBooks Pro® assigns you. It isn't law or IRS regulation to use a number format, so if you end up setting up your Chart of Accounts without a numbering format and only the account name, that is absolutely fine as well. Chart of Account numbers are used for internal control; they are never duplicated on a Federal or State Tax Return. Some clients prefer to see the account name only, and a number will only confuse them. Use your best judgment by getting to know your client's likes and dislikes. Remember, as you're creating or editing your chart of accounts, to apply them to the correct account classification! One of the biggest problems I see when people are setting up accounting software of any kind is that they don't set up their accounts correctly. Here is a mindless question: when setting up a checking account, what would you classify it under? Bank/Cash? You would be surprised, I have actually seen it listed under Fixed Assets, occasionally Liabilities, and once a client had it under Expenses. It is not because these people are idiots; it's because they don't know how to properly set up their books. That's why they need you. Make sure that you're putting your Accounts Receivable under Accounts Receivable and your Accounts Payable under Current Liabilities. As soon as you print out a balance sheet, you will be able to tell where your errors are if you have any. Just a word to the wise. You don't want to make mistakes like that and submit the reports to your clients. That would be really embarrassing.

After you're done creating your chart of accounts, you can start entering in the expenses that you have incurred so far. If you are using your personal cash or checking account, you will need to debit the expense that the payment is applied to, such as Office Supplies, and credit your Equity account – Capital Contributions, if that is where the money came from. You want to see how much money you are putting into your business, and if you don't track it the correct way, you will never know. The easiest way to do this without making a journal entry and without really having a good description of what the expense was or who it was paid out to, is by going directly to your capital contribution equity account in QuickBooks®. Double-click on the account to open it up. Just like in the checkbook register in QuickBooks®, all accounts look like a register. It would be a lot cleaner on your own financial reports to have a detailed listing of who you paid your expenses to. Enter the expenses that were paid by you to support your company in this account.

If you are using a credit card to start up your company, just create a liability account for "Credit Cards." Make sure you list each credit card that you will be using for this company as a sub-account. That way you can have a grand total of your credit liability along with each breakdown necessary. Also remember, with QuickBooks Pro®, you can reconcile even Credit Card Accounts! When you receive your monthly statement, reconcile it towards all of the entries you made to that particular account, and the interest is now tax deductible! Apply the interest to your expense account so you can recover that cost when you file your taxes. Try to designate one credit card to business only. Steer clear of using credit cards between both your personal and business life. I actually took one of my daughter's stickers that had letters, and put a deco silver B on one of my credit cards so I don't forget that the B is used for business expenses only. It makes for an easier life not having to sort through hundreds of credit card charges and receipts just to find the one that I used for business.

Once you are able to open a checking account for your business, you can start writing checks directly through your QuickBooks® checking chart of account, but in the meantime, you need to track everything through your equity account so you can take the deduction without forgetting about it when it comes time to do your taxes. After your business account is open and you have to deposit money from your personal account to cover business bills, the deposit entry would come from your Capital Contribution account to your business checking account. Wells Fargo® is the most convenient online bank that I have found. When you sign up for online banking, you can add all accounts, whether business or personal, that are connected to your Social Security number and transfer money between the accounts without having to handwrite a check and go to the bank to deposit it. What a great invention! FDIC does regulate the number of wire transfers and online transfers that you can do per month.

If you already own your vehicle without a monthly loan payment, the only suggestion is to take the mileage deduction. If you have a loan payment on your car, and the depreciation, gasoline, registration, and insurance exceed the standard mileage deduction of 0.36 cents per mile, then start using those expenses towards your business. You can also amortize your auto loan to recover the interest on the loan as well. Keep in mind though, whether or not you take all of the expenses and depreciation associated with your car, or just the standard mileage deduction, <u>you still need to make a mileage log!</u> If you do not furnish this information and you are involved in an audit, you <u>will lose</u> that deduction!

When you are bringing in new clients, you can customize your invoices on QuickBooks Pro® to your specific needs. You can set up sub-accounts on your income as well, to see where the majority of your revenue is coming from. I had mine set up to break down Audits, On-Site Bookkeeping, General Accounting, Fraud and Taxes.

QuickBooks Pro® also has time tracking. Peachtree® has Timeslips, but it is separate software from Peachtree®. This is very convenient for accountants and attorneys who bill for their time. You can keep track of how long you're spending on a particular client by logging on the time sheet as soon as you're finished with your work for that day. When you are ready to bill that client, you only need to select Time box on the invoice and you can click on each day and time duration that you want to bill that client for. This will also help you tremendously if you pick up any clients who are attorneys. As we all know, they bill for everything . . .

When paying bills or entering cash expenses that you charge back to your client (such as postage, telephone calls and photocopies), you can track this in QuickBooks Pro®. Just select the customer in the correct bill or check payment field, and it will automatically apply that expense to the correct client data file. When you are ready to invoice that client, click on Time/Costs and select your expenses; it will insert the costs onto your invoice when billing your client.

If you have other assets that you are now using for your business such as a desk, computer, or any other general-purpose office supply, you can write it off by depreciating it over its useful life. Say you paid $250 for a fax machine the prior year and now its sole purpose is for your new company. Technically you placed the fax in service on the date the company was opened, its value is listed at $250, and you can depreciate it over five years. You would make a journal entry that would debit your Fixed Asset account, and credit your Capital Contribution account. You would then depreciate the asset at the end of the fiscal year on your tax return unless you are a Corporation. Don't forget about the handy **Section 179 Deduction!** This deduction allows you to fully depreciate an asset (except real estate or a luxury car *see IRS guidelines*) up to $24,000 per tax year! Right now the IRS is allowing up to $100,000 for the next few years. Trust me; you'll get good at finding the best possible deductions when preparing your taxes along with your clients! Also, don't forget that you can now write off the business use of your home to help lower your business tax liability at the end of the year. If the room you are using has 250 square feet, you can write off the entire room as long as you are using it entirely for your business. If you are storing client files and reports in your garage, you can measure the area you are storing the documents in, and include that in your business use of the home as well. My advice is, if you're ever audited, and you have extra clothes hanging in the closet in your office, don't calculate that area in your business use. The IRS won't allow you to take the entire office if you have any personal items stored in there. This deduction will be taken on your Schedule C portion of your 1040 tax return, not reflecting on your profit & loss statement.

Now that you are self-employed, you have the liability of paying self-employment tax on your 1040 Schedule C tax return. There is a minimum earnings of $400 profit. If you earn a profit of more than $400, you must pay your FICA and Medicare, which is now called Self-Employment Tax. This is 15.3% of your profitable earnings. If you're earning $52,000 per year now, and your business expenses are roughly $15,000, your Self-Employment Tax liability will be roughly $5,661 for the year. ($52,000 minus $15,000 = $37,000 x 15.3% = $5,661). You are not allowed to take your itemized deductions before this tax is calculated. That being said, I cannot stress enough the importance of paying your quarterly taxes! I always budget my clients' payments by taking 18% off the top of each check received, putting it into an interest-bearing money market account, and using it for my quarterly tax payments. You do not want to get into a situation where you owe the IRS or State. If you set up a system and budget now, it won't financially hurt you later. Face it, we all have to pay our taxes, and just because you are self-employed now, doesn't mean that you do not have a tax liability any longer.

I briefly mentioned before the budget spreadsheet that I have included with this book. Here is where you need to evaluate your personal and business expenses. I cannot stress enough how important it is to look six to twelve months into the future and budget how you are going to survive and support yourself. I have included a budget and a cash flow schedule that can be modified in Excel or Works for you to play around with. You need to know how long your savings or even credit is going to carry you without earning as much money as you thought you would. The formulas are already calculated, so go through the budget and enter in your monthly expenses, business and personal. See what it takes for you to make it, so you are not caught off guard with any unforeseen surprises. Circumstances happen. I don't care who buys this book, there will be times when clients can't pay, they pay late, or you lose clients because they fold. Sometimes you have dry spells, when you aren't getting any calls. Who is going to support your mortgage payment during this time? Make sure you figure out how you are going to do this. This is where I have said, even I didn't quit my day job. If you are at a dry spell and are becoming concerned that you are not busy or earning enough money, and if you do not want to give up on your own business, the best solution would be to work temp until more clients come in. There is absolutely nothing wrong with calling Kelly Temporary Services to keep you busy on your down time. Make absolutely sure that you tell them you work part-time for another bookkeeping service. The reason I suggest that you inform them of employment with a bookkeeping service is that you don't want to be put in a situation where they think you are trying to steal their clients. If you must work temp, keep a low profile on the fact that you own the bookkeeping service. That means, don't tell the temporary agency or their clients. Above all, do not try to solicit their clients that you temp for. Just do your job, earn a paycheck and still give yourself time to solicit more work through your business. If you delegate your time properly, there will still be enough time to return client phone calls and work on other clients' bookkeeping needs. Just think of going to a temp assignment the same as going to a client's office. If you have to go there every Tuesday and Thursday for eight hours, let your clients know that if they need to get a hold of you, you are at another client's office on those days and will get back to them as soon as possible. Remember, you cannot earn top dollar working temp; the temp agency is charging top dollar for you, and so they will most likely pay you between $12 to $17 per hour depending on your level of experience and what the client is willing to pay for you. Generally the client will pay the temp agency anywhere from $22 to $27 per hour for a bookkeeper and junior accountant. Do not accept full-time employment from the temp agencies or their clients if you intend on working for yourself!

Make sure you have your company books in perfect order, and you feel comfortable in the way you were able to set them up. Once you feel you have a strong concept of how you need to approach setting up other companies' books, you can begin your sales and contacts.

The following page is just an assumption of what the startup costs of your bookkeeping business could be. The costs are minimal, and remember, you have better odds with yourself than you do trying to invest in the stock market or relying on punching someone else's time clock!

A-1 Bookkeeping

Budget Analysis

Startup Costs

Business License	$ 25.00
Ficticious Business Name	$ 20.00
Office Supplies	$ 75.00
Vello Bind Equipment	$ 130.00
Business Cards	$ 45.00
How-To Book	$ 69.95
QB Pro Advisor	$ 400.00
Checking Account	$ 9.00 (monthly)
Phone Line	$ 25.00 (monthly)
Cell Phone	$ 39.00 (monthly)
P.O. Box (6 months)	$ 40.00
Ten Key	$ 70.00
Desk	$ 250.00
Computer	$1250.00
Internet Access	$ 29.95 (monthly)
Total Expenses	$2477.90

Like millions of households, you probably already have your own computer and desk, so an average or accurate assumption of your initial startup costs are a minimal $978. Not bad for an investment that you have control over, is it?

This budget is just a general assumption of startup costs; also consider location and inflation expenses.

Chapter 2
Sales and Marketing

The Sales Process and Valuable Contacts

The most common question I've been asked to include in the 2nd Edition of this book was "What to say" to the contacts that are listed below. More specifically: How do you approach the networking resources, and what's the best thing to do or say to get in the door? The following list of resources will now have more detail on getting your foot in the door. Contacts are <u>very</u> important! Always think about whether you could benefit from someone else's type of business, and vice-versa! It doesn't matter where you go, or who you will come in contact with. There is always someone who is involved in some way or another with contacting people. I am going to list an incredible source for finding those clients. These resources are priceless considering the amount of work that I have generated from them. I have been at a point where I actually have to refer these clients to my sources because I was so overloaded with work! There will always be a need for your type of service. Do you ever wonder about the flat tax proposal, and how it could take away business from you as a bookkeeper or accountant? Let me ask you, logically and realistically, if it were to pass, do you think you would be able to buy a house, get a business loan, or even buy a car if you didn't have the proper financial information for your bank? Big retail outlets require financial statements before they will even consider carrying a product that your client may want to sell. The list will go on and on. Take notes, and as you're reviewing this list, write down people you know. You never know who you might think of that can bring you that client!

✓ **Number One Resource – Payroll Service Companies**

I will tell you time and time again, not to bite the hand that feeds you. Paychex and ADP are the US leader in payroll. They are also the number one resource for referrals and business. Smaller payroll companies are also hungry and aggressive for growth, so the networking is invaluable. Paychex relies specifically on two key factors in obtaining their business: one being their sales force, and two being accountants and bookkeepers. They do not pay for advertising. If you haven't noticed or paid close attention, take note that you won't see TV commercials, print ads or radio ads. They spend their advertising dollar on their inside sales reps to have literature, tri-folds, resource books and promo packages not only for the clients, but for us. They <u>need</u> you just as much as you need them. Tell that to Chris Whitte, my new Paychex rep, because Dawn was moved too far up north from me. He even brings me cookies when he knows I try not to eat junk food! Okay, this is just a plug for him; I promised that I would write about him in this book because he had hurt feelings that Dawn was in my other book. She'll be in every book I write! She was the key to my success and thus ten years later we have a wonderful friendship! Dawn (actually a head rep at Paychex for many years) was offered to start up Advantage Payroll Services in San Diego. She did, with full force, and they ended up having the highest growth and sales rate for the entire US. Paychex ended up buying Advantage because of the growth and competition factor. Dawn went back to Paychex, but is so good at sales and marketing that she was offered to start up CompuPay, so keep a lookout for CompuPay as well. Key reps will be heading up this payroll company! There is a common consensus in the accounting and bookkeeping industry, which is trust. I'll be the first to tell you that it is 100% more difficult to get that first client by cold calling and advertising. They don't know you from Adam, so why should the small business owner trust you with their money? Because you have a pretty tri-fold with foil embossed business cards? That may say something about your taste and budget, but it says nothing about your ability and integrity. The hardest part of getting business is becoming known. For someone else to drop your name and business card in conversation makes all the difference in the world! You need to figure out how not to be the "new" name. We all know that your main source of business will come from a payroll company, but "What do you say" to get in? In the back of this book is a contact and resource page where Paychex, Advantage and ADP Sales offices are located. Keep in mind that you **<u>don't</u>** have to hold 100% loyalty to just one payroll company. They don't hold 100% loyalty to just passing only your card out; they may have four other bookkeepers or accountants that they refer at the same time. The more people you know, the more business you will get, and the same goes for them as well. Call all of the main payroll companies in your area.

Ask who the sales rep for your territory is. Territory is very important to sales reps. You don't want to overstep or start fights with the sales reps. When the rep answers the phone or you have to leave a message, make <u>sure</u> that you let the rep know that you own a bookkeeping/accounting service, but you <u>don't</u> do payroll. Schedule a meeting to go over your services as well as their services. If it's only about you, then you are not going to get an excited rep. If you include their services and needs in your conversation, they have gained something as well and it's not just a one-sided sales call. Your networking relationship is now born. Do this with all the companies that you want to network with. If you have a first impression with a rep that isn't so good, which will happen every now and then, go with your gut instinct and avoid networking with them. It is your choice, remember that! When you meet with the reps, make sure that you have a package, business cards, tri-folds or flyers. If they are going to refer you, they need to have something to refer you with. Before you leave this meeting, ask your rep what CPA they use or like to refer business to. This is very important! It will open another door because now <u>you</u> are dropping names.

You know a few industry specific contacts and now you are not the new name.
A quick list of payroll companies in my area is:
- ✓ Paychex, Inc.
- ✓ CompuPay
- ✓ Advantage Payroll Services (a Paychex company)
- ✓ ADP
- ✓ Payroll Advantage
- ✓ Payroll Express
- ✓ Primepay
- ✓ Payroll One

Keep this in the back of your mind when networking with an Internet-based payroll service company, not to knock Intuit® who has a good payroll service system – however, their main office is in Nevada, and unless you can go to lunch in Nevada, how are you going to meet the people they know? Visual contact is just as important in trying to sell yourself, and if you are in another state, it's going to be more difficult.

✓ **Number Two Resource – CPA Firms**

CPAs are the 2nd leader in referrals. How to find the right CPA depends on the type of networking resources that you associate yourself with. Utilize the same system with the CPA firm as the payroll service; don't put all of your eggs in one basket. There are normally at least 100 CPA firms in a moderately large city. Obviously the bigger city, the more there are, so the best place to find those CPAs that you want to work with is to ask around. I have already told you to ask your payroll rep, so if you have three payroll service companies that you refer out to your clients, now you have at least six CPA names because the payroll rep will give you at least two CPA names.

I just realized as I sit here and type that this sounds like a pyramid. In a way, I guess it is a pyramid of names, useful tools to help you grow your business. Ask your bank, your friends, your family and the additional resources listed below for the names of the CPAs that they use as well as refer. Put together a very impressive resume, along with your flyer, business cards and/or tri-fold, and call the CPAs that you were referred to. Introduce yourself and tell them that they were referred to you by Chris at Paychex, or whoever sent you their way. Let them know what services you provide, and make sure you let them know that you don't do taxes. The CPA, just like the payroll company, needs to know that there is something in it for them as well. A CPA is not going to give you business if he or she knows that you do everything. If you know how to do taxes and become licensed, and specifically want to do them, sending a CPA some of your tax clients and not telling them that you do taxes too will bring you more work from the CPA. It is a definite asset for the CPA as well as you, that you know how to prepare and understand taxes, but knowing how and wanting to do them are two different things. I've prepared taxes for over ten years – Corporate, Individual and Partnerships. I stay up to date on the tax laws because I need to know just as much as the next guy. I now only prepare select client tax returns because I can honestly tell you, I don't like it. I don't like the crunch time between January 1st and April 15th, then the stress of the client with the big look of "duh" on their face when you've been telling them all year to pay in and they didn't. It isn't worth me going home with an ulcer over, so I chose to network taxes to someone who wants the stress and to give myself projects that are more fun such as financial crimes and business plans. So calling a CPA that was referred to you by one of your networking resources and inviting them to lunch will get you a foot in the door a lot quicker because you know someone they know. Make sure you ask the CPA for their prices so you know what it could cost your clients. Generally, CPAs charge from $125 to $250 per hour depending on what area of the United States you live in.

When you work with a CPA firm, make sure, no matter what the circumstances, that you never steal clients away! That is extremely bad business, and you will lose your reputation over it! CPA firms are an <u>excellent</u> source for <u>on-site</u> bookkeeping. A CPA firm always has clients that need on-site bookkeeping. It is usually a one-day-a-week, eight-hours-per-day job. That would mean each on-site job that you landed, you would earn between $140 and $240 per day. CPA firms generally won't refer you to do month-end accounting functions; it is mainly on-site bookkeeping service. The CPA won't want to give you <u>their</u> business, but on the flip side, their clients don't want to pay between $125 and $250 <u>per hour</u> for bookkeeping. That is why <u>they need you!!!</u> They still continue to do their clients' monthly financial statements, and tax returns, yet they keep their clients happy by supplying them with a reputable bookkeeper that costs much less than their rate. Everyone is happy! It is also not uncommon (and will most likely happen) that the CPA will require you to bill them and not their client. The reason is that the CPA will in return bill their client with a markup on your hourly rate. If your rate is $25 per hour, the CPA will most likely charge their client $35 to $40 per hour for your time. Don't feel like you're not getting enough money per hour. I do it because you call me with questions that I can't always bill the client for, so covering my additional time by increasing the cost per hour from your bill doesn't leave me showing a loss with my un-billable time. If the client is your client and you have the CPA prepare the income tax return, you could either have the CPA bill you directly so you could add a small markup for running the information, or you could have the CPA bill directly to the client. That would be entirely up to you and how comfortable you were with making sure your client paid you on time so you could pay the CPA.

If you are a CPA purchasing this book to learn how to open your own CPA firm, the principles in finding clients are the same. Instead of you being the number two resource for referrals, the bookkeeper in this case would be your number two resource in referrals. Instead of offering bookkeeping services, you need to put together what services you provide, what is your specialty and what type of accounting you want to do. Whether it's Taxes, Tax Planning, Audits, Financial Business Plan Write-Ups or General Monthly Financials, you are still greatly needed by the Payroll companies, forms companies and bookkeepers.

✓ Number Three Resource – Bookkeeping Forms Companies

Believe it or not, companies that sell checks, invoices, computer forms, and other accounting and bookkeeping supplies are an excellent resource for referrals and clients! A good portion of my business when I first started came from McBee Bookkeeping Systems. They were the company that my Paychex Rep referred to me. My clients always had a need for computer checks, so I would call my representative at McBee and she would give me a 40% accountant's discount! Plus she gave my company a starter kit with checks included for free! The only downside to this is that companies like McBee and even QuickBooks® can't beat the cost for checks at checkfamous. However, with the referrals and networking resources that you will gain from McBee, paying an additional $25 for your checks is well worth it especially if you get clients from them. You need to think of the possibility of revenue and if it's worth it for you. When you are first starting out with your business and you don't have any real income coming in, ordering discounted printing is okay to get you going, but think of the long-term relationship when you order your next set of checks. To list a few of the companies related to the number three resource:

✓ McBee Bookkeeping Systems (Nationwide)

- ✓ Office Depot (Nationwide)
- ✓ Staples (Nationwide)
- ✓ Office Max (Nationwide)
- ✓ Local Office Supply Stores

You will get more referrals from companies like McBee than from your general office supply store because some companies don't allow their employees to refer people because of the liability issues. When contacting stores like Office Depot, generally the person you are going to contact is the person in the software department who is selling QuickBooks®. The one downfall for an office supply store is they go through sales people and managers rather quickly. There isn't a reciprocated service between you and an Office Depot like there is with you, Paychex, and CPAs R Us. If you go into a store enough times and become a recognized face, starting a conversation with the manager or software salesman is normal. You don't need to push your business on them, just briefly mention what you do and let them ask you questions. If you offer advice and help you're more likely to get a response from someone at the store. If Joe is buying QuickBooks® for his Web Design company and asks the salesman if he knows of anyone who could help set it up because it looks too overwhelming, your card or tri-fold could be the first thing they think of to give to Joe. The uncomfortable part is asking them to pass out your card if someone asks for help with QuickBooks® or other accounting software, but if you're comfortable just go for it.

✓ Number Four Resource – Banks

The banking industry is so cutthroat in today's business world that banks like Union Bank of California hired a specific staff to call accountants and bookkeepers in their immediate vicinity to solicit a networking program. Go to your bank, the one you opened your business account with. Talk to your New Accounts banker and use the same principle as all the others. There has to be something the bank can get in return: namely, customers – especially customers who need business loans, lines of credit, home equity loans and bank accounts. You should specifically target banks that provide SBA Loans. Generally people wanting to open a new business or purchase an existing business require SBA funding to do this. They are usually qualified for one specific function but don't know beans about bookkeeping or accounting. Also ask your Paychex or ADP rep which bank they network with. Ask for a business card, and once again, when you call Yvonne at Wells Fargo, tell her that Chris at Paychex referred you. They're just like you, they need the work, and without the work there won't be money.

A General List of Businesses that relate to your services.

Workers Compensation Insurance Companies – They carry the insurance policies for Workers Compensation. They are a very good resource for clients. They see how the books are kept while preparing an audit. If they feel the client has a situation at hand where their books are a complete disaster, they can refer you. You in return can refer a Payroll Service, CPA Firm and a Bookkeeping Forms Company. The list can go on and on. Word of mouth works wonders. Not to jump to a different topic but 100% of my work came from these referrals that I am sharing with you. I have never done any type of advertising, marketing or even soliciting. That doesn't mean that you shouldn't. I think that you need to proceed with every reliable resource to become successful. I was just fortunate to find the right people to promote my business to.

Insurance Companies – Target the ones that provide Business Insurance, General Liability, Auto, Professional and Bond Insurance. The best way to get your feet in the door with these companies is to contact them when you are price shopping for your client's insurance needs.

Investment Brokers – You would be surprised by the referrals you could receive from an Investment Broker. They deal with businesses that are looking for 401k's, Employee Profit Sharing, and additional investment packages. I have received many solicitations and phone calls from Investment Brokers to obtain my business for those related items when I was working for someone else.

Health Insurance Companies – They are trying to find clients just like you are, promoting their health insurance to businesses. They are a very good resource for business referrals.

31

IRS or State Auditors – Believe it or not, IRS and State Agents hate to begin an Audit with a business owner who literally has a box of receipts. In this book, I will explain how to prepare an Audit package for your client to present to the IRS that can save your client a great deal of money. Try to meet with an agent and let them know what you can do to help make their job easier.

Law Firms – About 80% of the time there are small Law Firm practices located within a bigger firm just leasing office space. They tend to do all of their billing and accounting themselves. Because they charge at least $150 per hour, that is valuable time wasted billing clients and paying bills, when they could pay you to do everything in just one day per week. Two of my clients were Law Firms; one I did the Audit for, as well as Financial Investigations. Lawyers can keep you very busy! The reason is that they charge such a high hourly rate; $40 per hour to them is minimal. But it takes them almost twice as long as you to complete all of their bookkeeping needs; you could complete the work in half the time. Let's say it takes an attorney twelve hours (1 ½ days) to complete everything, and it takes you eight hours. They have wasted $1,800 per week in their billable time when they could have paid you $320 to do the work quicker and most likely more efficiently.

✓ Other resources

Look in the newspaper for Part Time Bookkeeping. You can submit a letter along with a resume to the company searching for a bookkeeper, explaining how they can save on Workers Compensation, Federal and State Taxes, and get the high quality of work from a "Professional." Think of the breakdown this way. When a small business owner hires an employee, it comes with baggage such as Workers Comp, Unemployment and Payroll Taxes that they must deal with, as well as an employee's state of mind. This is not always in the best interest of the employer. When you hire a "Sub-Contractor," they have a different state of mind because the Sub-Contractor owns their company. They are the reason why they may or may not eat next week. Which means more productive work for the Small Business Owner. The self-employed individual (you) is much more capable of wanting to do the job compared to an employee who expects to get paid because they show up. The other expectation is that a professional who does this every day for a half dozen other clients is more proficient and won't take as long as an employee who will always try to milk the time clock. So in all actuality, when you have a bookkeeper who works part-time, 20 hours per week, they have in their mentality that the 20 hours per week has to be met because at $10 to $15 per hour they can't afford any minute less. So they will make the job take a long time. When you go in to your client's office, you look at the pile of papers and say with a more realistic analysis that it should only take you 10 hours to complete because you don't need to make the job last long. So for Mr. Small Business Owner, that 20-hour per week job at $15 per hour costs him $300 per week in wages, plus 7.65% in FICA/Medicare, plus 3.4% in State Unemployment (depending on your state), .08% in Federal Unemployment, and another 1.5% in Workers Compensation. That $300-per-week employee realistically costs the Small Business Owner $340 per week. You come in and can get the job done in 10 hours, alleviating Workers Comp, Unemployment, FICA/Medicare and company politics. You're more professional, you want the client and will service them better, so your bill is only $250 per week ($25 per hour x 10 hours). You're already saving the client $115 per week. Explaining that to a potential client in simplified terms will get more of a response and a greater possibility of landing a new client.

Place advertisements in your local newspaper and employment newspapers. If someone is going through an audit, you could place an ad regarding your abilities to organize and compile financial statements for Audits. Make sure that you inform the client when they call that you can correspond with the Auditor; however you are not allowed to be present at a trial because you are not a CPA or an Enrolled Agent, unless otherwise required to testify by the IRS. Also place your other services in the ad as well. Never put your prices in the ad! Let the client meet you even if it's over the phone, so you can build a comfort zone.

Look in the local newspaper for Fictitious Business Names posted. A lot of times, those are new businesses just starting out. You'll be amazed after reviewing that section of the newspaper, which one of your contacts calls you with a referral from one of the businesses listed.

The State Board of Equalization (Sales Tax in your state) sells a list of new businesses that have just applied for a Sales Tax Identification number. Contact your State Office to find out how you can purchase that list of new business names. This list will be fresher than any other new business list you could purchase, and the deliverability rate will be much better. Not all states offer this list.

If you decide that you want to go "door to door" so to speak, be advised that people don't like solicitors. It is completely different when you are referred to a potential client than if you just came in off the street. I can't stand solicitors! It's the hardest thing that I have to deal with in terms of my phone manners. I try to keep in mind that **my contacts are solicitors, and they are doing the hardest job for me**. They're getting their foot in the door, which could potentially bring me business as well. I guess my main setbacks are telephone solicitors who call you when you're finally sitting down to dinner with your family whom you haven't seen all day. Try to present yourself as UN-solicited as possible. If you call them, try to give them helpful information or resources, especially if they are a new business just starting out. I think that creating your own list of prospects is the hardest way to generate clients. But if it comes naturally to you, run with it!

✓ **Examples of Phone Conversations of what I say when I call new contacts or reps.**

First phone call to Paychex:

Julie: Hi, this is Julie at San Diego Business Accounting; may I speak with Dawn please?

Dawn: Hi, this is Dawn.

Julie: Hi Dawn, this is Julie Mucha, I own San Diego Business Accounting and was interested in getting some information on the types of payroll service and pricing that you offer. My services don't include payroll, and I want to make sure I have other resources for my clients.

Dawn: Sure, that would be great, would you like me to mail it, or come to your office?

Julie: I would like to get together so that we can meet; how would a lunch meeting sound? [If you offer a lunch meeting, you're buying! It's proper etiquette.]

Dawn: That would be great, how about Sammy's in Mission Valley....

First phone call to CPA:

Julie: Hi, this is Julie with San Diego Business Accounting; may I speak with Larry please?

Receptionist: Larry is not available, make I take a message or would you like his voice mail?

Julie: His voice mail, please.

Larry's voice mail: Hi Larry, this is Julie from San Diego Business Accounting [when naming yourself, think of a smaller name!]. I was referred to you by Dawn with Paychex. I own an Accounting Service, however I don't offer Tax Returns. I am looking for a CPA to whom I can send my clients' Year End Taxes, and you came highly recommended. If you are taking on new clients, please give me a call at 619-449-0675. I look forward to talking with you.

The ending to that story is Larry called me back, we discussed what services I just don't want to do anymore, taxes being one of them, we met for lunch, and I met a down-to-earth CPA who I get along great with. I work with a few other select CPAs in San Diego who do a great job and send me referrals.

Phone conversation with a new client, Sawdust:

Answering machine picks up:

Julie: Hi, this is Julie calling from Sullivan Business Services [that was my old company name – long story]. I was referred to you by Dawn with Paychex who informed me that you are looking for an accountant. Please give me a call at your earliest convenience. You can reach me at 619-449-0675

Sawdust: [Returns my call about a week later; I was so busy I forgot all about this referral. I don't ever recommend forgetting who you call!]

Julie: This is Julie.

Sawdust: Hi, this is Chris with Sawdust.

Julie: Sawdust, what do I need Sawdust for?

Sawdust: You called me . . .

Julie: Oh, I'm sorry, I thought you were a solicitor. Hi Chris, I hear you are in need of an accountant. What can I do for you?

Chris: I need help setting up QuickBooks®. I had someone in here, but they seemed to have messed it up. I am also looking for someone to set up specialized spreadsheets to track my jobs and to obtain a bank line of credit.

Julie: No problem; I specialize in QuickBooks, WIP Reports and Bank Financing. When is a good time to get together so I can see where your books are at right now?

This is actually a true story; luckily enough, Chris with Sawdust was forgiving enough to see me the following Friday and my services were retained. Remembering this phone call has been the source of many a good laugh because I apparently did need Sawdust after all. I ended up marrying him five years later!

✓ **Selling yourself to land the account**

You received the referral and you called the potential client to set up an interview. Now how do you land the account? I can only guide you in steps to take, mistakes to avoid, and conversations, but you are the one who will complete the circle. I can tell you that appearance is very important in selling your services! "Clean and professional" will guarantee you a foot in the door. Not everyone can go out and dress to the nines with designer suits, but clean, groomed and neat are acceptable descriptions when you are meeting with people. I have found over the years that with some clients I can wear shorts or jeans to their office because they are blue-collar workers. This, mind you, comes <u>after</u> the initial consultation. No need to wear nylons to an office where there is heavy equipment and machinery all over the office and shop. But if you have a client who is a lawyer, CPA or in a professional field where attire is important, you need to dress the part. Now, just a little personal advice from a third party that is not intentionally trying to hurt anyone's feelings. Before you go to any meeting with a network or referral client, brush your teeth! I know it sounds a bit presumptuous, but if you ever had a nice Carne Asada burrito for lunch with lots of

Salsa Fresca loaded with onions, your breath might need some help. First impressions are everything, and if something like that is the first thing a potential client remembers about you, then it could be a bad memory.

Cell phones are incredibly rude! Leave it in your car! If your phone rings during a meeting with someone and you answer it, you are telling the person you are with that their meeting with you has taken second place behind the person on the phone. If you did that at my meeting, I would never call you back. Proper phone etiquette also means no talking on a cell phone so everyone else can hear your conversation. Talking on cell phones in lines at grocery stores, banks, at a restaurant, or anyplace where you are the center of a large group of people is rude. Most cell phone plans have voice mail. If yours does not, invest the extra $10 per month to have voice mail attached to your cell phone so if the phone call is important, they can leave a message. You can also turn your ringer off and have the phone vibrate if you have missed a call. If you are concerned with missing a phone call that might be an emergency with your children, then nonchalantly look at the phone (after it vibrates because you turned the ringer off), see what number was missed on the Caller ID, and if it is a call from your babysitter or the school, excuse yourself to the restroom and return the call.

Do not be late to meetings! It looks very bad. If your appointment is at 10:00 a.m. and you don't know how to get there, leave early enough in case you get lost. It's always best to be early rather than being late. You can always wait in your car in the parking lot, jot down notes and to-do's, return a few phone calls, but don't be late.

Once you've won their trust to sell your services, your next step is **Confidence!** Like I said before, you are in a completely different ball game. You are no longer an Employee, but a Business Owner. You don't have to respond to anyone above you! It is completely different selling your services compared to trying to find a job. If you know what you're doing and give valuable comparison information along with how they should be running their bookkeeping to reach a more profitable business, they will listen. The first few consultations to prospective clients are filled with nerves. It's really no different than having the solo song in the school play. You get butterflies, maybe even a little stage fright, but wait, you already spoke to them on the phone, so that ice is broken. You know who they are and what they are looking for. That will give you a few days to prepare for the meeting, depending on when you make the appointment. When you prepare for your meetings, go through your notes on what they need. I have enclosed a Quote Sheet form for potential clients. This is a key form to go by to see what type of business they are, what their accounting activity is, and it will give you a basis to go by on what fees to charge. When you are doing the first initial phone consultation with the company, go down through each number and ask the questions to the client. When you are finished at the meeting, <u>tell</u> them how you can help their company become more profitable by showing them where they are spending too much money, or why their receivables look bad and how their records should look. Nine out of ten times, with your professional appearance, confidence, and profitable recommendations, you will land the account!

Do your homework! Study what you need to know from my forms and this book regarding questions to ask, and documentation you need to begin creating their books! If you're not sure about a question they ask, always find out where you can go to get that correct information! Let your client know that you will call them back as soon as possible with the answer! Never leave them hanging.

If you are prepared for what a client needs and wants, the meeting will be a lot more comfortable, and your confidence to speak to them will show. After the first few meetings the butterflies go away, and the confidence outweighs anything else! I guess in my decade of self-employment I tend to have the perspective that they need me, which is why they called or were referred. So for me, I am providing a solution for small business owners. Now that I am mainly focusing on Fraud and Financial Investigations, I am starting over, in a sense. I'm offering a completely different type of service to a different type of business resource. I am using the same principles from the first day I went out on my own, which is "How many people do I know, and what type of networking resource will get me the type of client base I desire?" Because people know my name and heard I am steering towards a different avenue of accounting, I am getting phone calls for Fraud. Had my resources not been so valuable, I would be back to square one with a "What do I do?" look on my face.

The subject matter of fees and rates will inevitably come up for discussion either during your first phone call or the first meeting. Rates are discussed in depth in Chapter 3; however, you need to know how to handle the bargaining client. If they tend to steer away because of your rate, stand your ground (politely). <u>Never</u> sell yourself short. Your services are worth X dollar amount and that is your rate. If you decide to give a discount rate for the first few months, that is fine, but make your client aware that your rate will increase to your normal fee! Include that in your proposal! If you lose an account because your rate is too high, another one will come that will agree with your fees. You cannot get professional quality service for nothing. Barter with your potential client by saying that anything less than X dollar amount will bring them poor sloppy service that they will need to be careful of. You can also assure them that if they do go that route, it's guaranteed that they will need either you or another more expensive bookkeeper in a few short months to fix the errors of the cheaper bookkeeper. I've done it many times! Don't let it affect your drive if you don't get a client every now and then. Trust me, these people don't know much about accounting, and they need you. They could either pay a CPA a substantial amount of money, or pay you a low $25 to $40 per hour to set them on the right track. You might have slow spells every now and then, but get your name out there and meet people; someone will drop your name and you will get referrals!

There are so many different types of clients that you could have. Each one needs a different service, yet the bottom line is, all of the general accounting services that you will be providing will be the same. I will give you a few examples of the type of services each client could require.

Bar – *Cash Basis* – Generally would require weekly A/P processing, posting cash receipts and maintaining checking accounts for up-to-date balance activity, budgeting for A/P processing, posting payroll and double-checking payroll and payroll tax accuracy. With monthly financial reports, quarterly SBA reports, year-end accounting and tax preparation, this client would most likely be handled at <u>your office</u>.

Retail Outlets – *Cash Basis* – Generally would require the same maintenance as a bar. My advice on retail, they are a lot more work than the service industry. The accounting and record keeping takes quite a bit longer, and the chances of audits are higher because the amount of cash that goes through the registers. A lot of accountants and bookkeeping services won't handle these types of clients just for that reason. It could work in your best interest, or not; I choose not to handle them, just to avoid a headache.

Law Firms – *Accrual Basis* – This type of client would be an on-site service. Would require up-to-date Accounts Receivable and collections to make sure their clients are paying in a timely manner. Would also require Accounts Payable, filing, payroll posting, reporting, monthly financial reports, quarterly financial reports, year-end tax preparation and reporting.

Service Industry – (Automotive, construction, manufacturer, etc.) *Accrual* – Could possibly be both on-site and off-site depending on services needed. They might just require monthly bookkeeping services, which would be at your office, or Accounts Payable and Receivable processing as well as job costing. This type of client would generally require quarterly bank reports as well as your monthly financials and year-end financial and tax processing.

Think of each business or industry as having the same fundamentals of accounting and record keeping, and trying to track their profit margins and assets in the same manner. They may be entirely different business types, but they all are operating under the same purpose. They want to see where they're making their money, and where they are losing their money. It is all really common sense, and before you know it, everything will click. Your ability to walk into a new client's business and feel confident in the information and documentation that you can provide them for their business, no matter what they do, will excel at an all-time high!

✓ **Marketing Ideas**

I have been learning myself, in hit-and-miss fashion, what type of marketing works and what does not. Just as in poker, everything is a gamble. What may work for me, might not work for you. So the only thing I can do is to merely suggest ideas. It's no secret that my business success has been based on my resources that I have listed in this book. However, I'll be the first to admit that my advertising and marketing skills have been mediocre, to say the least. I have this little thing with solicitors. I imagine I have been very biased. Well frankly, I think my one-sided opinion is based solely on the fact that I can't stand door-to-door sales people, or telemarketers. I do always appreciate the networking resources that are doing the hardest job for me! After successfully selling my "services," I was in many positions to sell "products," such as this book. But I didn't want to fail as I did with another venture, so I sought out the experts in the field. Through a chance encounter – I think it was my karma finally coming back around my way – I met Paul and Sarah Edwards. They are the home-based business King and Queen, with over 16 published books that touch on just about every subject related to successful Self-Employment and Life Coaching. I learned that Sarah Edwards offers an online course for non-marketing individuals such as myself, so I signed up. The course is $295 for 12 weeks and is based upon their book **"Getting Business to Come to You, 2nd Edition,"** available at Amazon.com or at book outlets. The book not only gives you incredible advice on what works and what doesn't, but opens your eyes to what you have been doing wrong. Advertising is an expensive lesson, especially if it doesn't work. You can spend thousands upon thousands of dollars throwing good money after bad money, and when you're trying to build a successful business, you're usually blind to your mistakes until it's too late. This online course goes through the chapters in their book, teaching you along the way. Sarah Edwards not only guides you through the process, she also reviews your ideas and work through weekly online posts to keep your enthusiasm up and going. She also helps you build a marketing plan and follows through with you as you are implementing it. I loved the course because it really opened my eyes to what I didn't like about advertising and marketing, and gave me options for what I do like. It makes you want to market, not dread it. It gives you cost-cutting ideas so you don't spend your entire bankroll guessing. I truly believe this course is well worth the small investment, and if you sign up, mention this book and Sarah Edwards will give you a 10% discount on the price. I have included a coupon with the 10% discount for the marketing course in the Additional Resource Chapter of this book. For more information, the website is located at: http://www.simplegoodlife.com

Postcard Mailers

The most cost-effective form of advertising that I have found for small promotions is Postcard Mailers. When you mail a tri-fold or brochure, the recipient has to open it, and the five-second rule applies. If you have not piqued their interest within the first five seconds, consider your mailer filed in the round file (trash can). With a post card, you have a mailer that is already opened. The best results are when you mail in triplicate. They say it takes at least three times of your advertisement being seen by a customer or client for them to respond to it. Postcards can be done inexpensively. There are many companies online that offer 5,000 postcards for $389. Local printing companies can't beat the online price of many of these postcard pieces. 5,000 postcards may seem a bit large in quantity if you are a small business not trying to gain 5,000 clients. I found a company in Florida that offered 2,500 postcards for $119. I was leery at first, but after my original printer had problems, I had no choice but to go elsewhere and take my chances. They printed three sets of 2,500 postcards and had them shipped to my door within 7 days. Florida to San Diego, not a bad turnaround time. The postcards were of excellent quality as well. I was very impressed. The company name is Online Print House and their website is located at www.onlineprinthouse.com. The postage, if put on by you, will cost 23 cents for each postcard. If you have a mailing that has more than 1,000 pieces, I suggest a meter, because it is very time-consuming and monotonous to put stamps on that many postcards. Mailing houses will put the postage and delivery address on the piece for an additional fee. Their fees are pretty expensive, so the more you do for yourself, the more you will save. Your mailing list can be purchased from a number of companies. I unfortunately had purchased a bad list. Generally, you would receive up to 10% of your mailing returned as undeliverable. My recent mailing was over 25% returned, which is totally unacceptable. I don't suggest buying a mailing list from Internet-based companies unless you are absolutely sure of their track record. Ask your networking contacts if they know any good list companies; look in your local phone book for list companies; then go online to your local Better Business Bureau and check them out. Make sure they don't have any complaints and then give them a call. A general new company list will cost you around 7 to 9 cents per name. If you want to use the list more than once, it will cost you about 15 cents per name. Depending on the complexity of the list (whether you want phone numbers, individual as well as company names, etc.) the cost could be more for each additional request. So if you wanted to send out a postcard mailer to 1,000 new companies that just opened up their doors, your cost for this marketing plan would run you about $400 for each mail, and mailing it the suggested three times would run you around $1,200 total. I do postcard mailers for my books. You have to get creative and have catchy phrases that will pique the interest of the individual you are sending it to. The three postcards for this book say on the front:

1.) I bet you've thought about opening your own Bookkeeping Service at least once.

2.) I bet you've thought about opening your own Bookkeeping Service another three times since our last chat.

3.) What are you waiting for? You don't have to quit your day job; get clients on the side and supplement your income!

You need to offer your target consumer something that will make them want to call you. Most people want a discount of some kind. If you offered your potential client two free hours of QuickBooks® training they might be more excited to call you than if you just let them know you do bookkeeping down the street. If your main service is going to be onsite bookkeeping, offer them a few hours of free time on their first invoice. Word it in a way that entices them to call you to find out what you do. You can find a graphic artist who will help you put together a professional-looking postcard as well as your stationary. My graphic artist does an awesome job. She designed my logos, the book covers, my postcards and all of my stationary. She does do work all over the US via the Internet as well. There is link information in the contact page of this book and a banner on my links page to find her. The name of the company is Urick Designs. Kinko's can also help you design a postcard mailer.

Websites

In this day and age, if you are not Web-based then you are behind the times. All the Internet really is, is an incredibly large encyclopedia. People, including you, go on the Internet to look for information. Keep in mind that the new client isn't going to go searching for you on the Internet; they're going to go searching for QuickBooks® help, in which case, if you are a Certified Pro Advisor, they will find you. If you have a website link from Intuits® Pro Advisor site, they will find out more about you: what you do, who you are, how to get a hold of you. Very few small business owners will have the time or patience to go searching the Internet for some inexpensive backwoods bookkeeping shop. Would you? Unless someone directs them to your website via certification such as Intuit®, they don't know who you are. Money is a very personal subject. That is why it's 100% easier to get clients by referrals than by cold calling. I'm not saying that you won't get any business straight from someone going to your website; I'm saying it is just as difficult as going door to door when no one knows who you are. Your clients however will appreciate a website that has information that they can use, such as links to help them find out how to get IRS Forms, Tax Deadlines and more. It helps also to have a simple way of contacting you, via email, because they don't feel like making a phone call. We all get like that, every once in a while. What a nice invention email has turned out to be! So my suggestion is, don't waste your bankroll on an expensive website unless you are absolutely sure it will make you money by bringing you clients.

There are many websites that have free design templates. You need to know how to make a Web page if you want to save some money. You can hire many companies to build your website which can get costly, but that's what they specialize in. The best software to use to build your own website is FrontPage. It is a Microsoft®-based product (well, everything is a Microsoft®-based product, isn't it?) that I use to create my own Web pages. It has taken years of trial and error to figure out shopping carts, merchant accounts, graphics, links and the whole nine yards, and that is another book . . . not mine. You can save yourself the aggravation by letting Intuit build a Web page for you as part of their QuickBooks® and Pro-Advisor package. It is additional, but they do have special promotions. Check with them when you sign up to be a Pro-

Advisor because their promotions are constantly changing and I don't want to have to keep updating this book just for an Intuit® promo. If you have the knowledge and experience in creating a Web page, and are looking for free Web templates, try www.27stars.com or www.fuzzywebmaster.com. They have many good templates for free, plus additional templates that you would pay for. Depending on what your budget is, make sure you have enough to survive on before you go out and start investing in Web pages. You can also use the free site submission services that you go to once a month to submit your website to major search engines. If you do it once a month, you will get your website some free search engine advertising. The best sites I've found for this are www.addpro.com and www.freewebsubmission.com. They submit your site to about 30 major search engines at a time. They just want a reciprocal link from your website to theirs. Put it on your links page; it's worth it. You can register a domain at www.cheap-domainregistration.com, which is about the most inexpensive site to register a domain. The costs range from $4.95 to $8.95 to register for one year. Your web hosting is the company who you will be storing your website with on their server. Because an Accounting and Bookkeeping Service does not have a great deal of pages and images, you don't need to go out and find a hosting company with a billion bells and whistles. You can find web hosts for as little as $3.95 per month. A good Web Hosting company that I know of is www.bizland.com, or even cheap-domainregistration.com has a Web-hosting plan for as little as $3.95 per month, which is cost-effective Web hosting that won't break your bank. You can even find free Web hosting companies. I did it for a while, but found it to be incredibly tacky. Banners filled the top portion of my Web pages because the free hosting service meant that you would display their banner adds throughout every portion of your website. Sometimes it's best to just pay a few dollars a month to avoid any such inconvenience.

Marketing Materials

A tri-fold or brochure is a wonderful tool to have to give to networking contacts, as well as to mail out to a potential client who calls you and asks for some literature about you and your service. Even Kinko's can help you design a nice-looking tri-fold relatively inexpensively. There is a company in New York called Vista Print. They are an online service that not only prints tri-folds, but also business cards, letterhead and just about everything. They have templates that you can choose from, just adding your text describing your business and services. They offer templates for tri-folds, brochures, business cards, letterhead and even postcards. Their web address is **www.vistaprint.com.**

You can print business cards from your own personal computer and printer, but I will be quite honest with you – it does look a bit low-budget. You want to make a good first impression, and even with a business card, it does say a lot about you. If you really weigh the cost of printing your own business cards versus having a print shop do it for you, you won't be saving much money. The paper to print the cards is already costing at least $19 because they are perforated, then the ink to print the cards, and what about the software? That is only for 250 business cards, but you probably ran out of ink before you used all of the paper. You can do it in Microsoft Word, but who needs another job just to try and make the printer line up with the box! Save yourself the aggravation by finding someone to print business cards for you. Kinko's will do business cards as well, or go online to Vistaprint and see if you like a design from their templates. They even have separate designs for accountants and bookkeepers!

The best possible package you could give to your networking group would be a nice-looking folder that matches a color in your business card. When you start making more money, you can order pre-printed embossed folders with your company name and contact information. But for now, a nice-colored folder that can hold a business card, tri-fold and introduction letter to whomever you are delivering the package will do. When designing your tri-fold or brochure, include all the services that you provide, and add a nice description of your specialties, but never put your price! Price always goes in an engagement letter! Don't make your literature too overwhelming or full of unnecessary details and explanations. Small businesses like simple translation. Write something that will give them an overall idea of who you are and what you provide. You can include a small bio on the back page if you feel comfortable with that, but make sure you include a Mission Statement. What is your mission with your clients?

My mission is: *To create a solution for the small business owner's accounting needs by implementing internal controls for fraud prevention as well as financial growth.*

Ask yourself what your goal and intention is, then apply it to a nice Mission Statement. It will give you a bit more worth as well as a goal to strive for.

Flyers are a good way to offer a discount or special for your services, to get your foot in the door. Make sure your flyer isn't too busy, and that it gives the potential client a reason why they should call you. Most people call on a solicitation when there is something in it for them. You could offer 25% off a QuickBooks® install and setup, $20 off Tax Preparation services, or one free hour of bookkeeping services. You need to use your own judgment on what you feel is worth it. If you gave them 25% off a QuickBooks® install, the probability of you having them as a monthly client is a lot greater than just a one-time shot. They will end up calling you every time they have a QuickBooks® problem, which is billable time for you. It needs to benefit you too, and once you start getting more clients than you can handle, you won't need to offer discounts to get in the door.

Joining Local Organizations

To be well known throughout your community, it is normally a good idea to join local organizations such as the Chamber of Commerce and the Better Business Bureau. These organizations are expensive, so if you don't need to join all of them at once, pick and choose. The best bet is the BBB because it gives you an endorsement of sorts, stating that you are agreeing to abide by all business ethics and won't do anything illegal to jeopardize your standing with their organization. The Chamber of Commerce, as well as the local BBB office in your area, has chapter meetings where you can go meet people and network. It is a good resource to find business. Here is a little word of advice about joining too many organizations: you will eventually become so busy with all your newfound responsibilities that your home life and client list will eventually suffer because you promised more than you can handle.

Always remember . . . It's who you know and who knows you.

Chapter 3
Bookkeeping Services

✓ **Service Types**

There are many different types of services that a bookkeeping company can provide. A lot depends on how much business you want to give to your networking resources. The two biggest resources are payroll and CPA firms, meaning that generally you would not offer payroll or taxes for your client because you would have the companies that specialize in just that area do it. It would be very hard for you to compete with the rates of a payroll service company anyway, and a CPA has more experience and knowledge in tax breaks than a small bookkeeping service. However, that does not mean that you can't do it. Some clients will not want a payroll service. They might feel too many people are involved. The general services that an accounting/bookkeeping service offers are as follows:

✓ **Write-Up Services**

Write-Up services are for small businesses that are too large for the owner to gather the financial information for the tax return just once a year, yet too small to hire full-charge bookkeeper. These write-up services work this way: you go to the client's office to pick up their bookkeeping information such as Checkbook Registers, Canceled Checks, Bank Statements, Invoices, Deposits, Payroll Records and Vendor Bills. You would then take them back to your office and input the data into your accounting system (QuickBooks) then review the data you entered by printing financial reports. Check it for errors and then finalize the financial reports in a professional portfolio, then deliver the data supplied by your clients along with their finalized financial reports. Write-Up services also include preparing Sales Tax Returns, Quarterly Payroll Tax Returns (if you offer payroll), Year-End 1099's and Year-End closed out books. Write-Up services can be done monthly, quarterly and bi-annually. This helps the small business owner know where they stand financially throughout the year without having to hire an in-house bookkeeper. They also don't want the added expense of buying a computer, so they normally hand-write all of their checks and invoices. The best description of a write-up client is one who drops you a shoebox filled with receipts and canceled checks and says here you go, tell me how I'm doing. Write-Up services could also include a client who has QuickBooks® and an in-house bookkeeper who pays the bills and invoices clients. The bookkeeper will then prepare all of the information that you need (monthly client checklist), send it over to your office with an Accountant Back-up of QuickBooks, have you review, fix mistakes, make journal entries, and finalize the financial statements. You would then import the accountant's changes to the client's computer, deliver the finalized financial reports, and do it again the next month. If you have a very unorganized client, it is best if you provide them with a filing system so that they can organize their data. The best system is an accordion file, whether it's the brown tabbed accordion that is separated by alphabetical order, or a box that has hanging files in it labeled by alphabetical order. The office supply stores also have the accordion folders that are separated by bookkeeping and tax information; those are the best to use. They will cost you around $15, but your client will appreciate it. When I prepare Write-Up services, I charge by the hour, but it is common for bookkeeping services to charge a set monthly fee. Generally a small client that doesn't have a great deal of activity is charged a minimum monthly fee of $100. When offering a Write-Up Service, the financial reports that you will need to provide to your client are as follows:

Financial Reports

Balance Sheet

Monthly Profit and Loss Statement

Quarterly Profit and Loss Statement

YTD Profit and Loss Statement

WIP Report (Work in Progress or Job Profitability)

Cash Flow Forecast

Trial Balance

Accounts Payable Aging (Unpaid Bills Detail)

Accounts Receivable Aging (Open Invoices)

Payroll Reports

General Ledger Reports

✓ On-Site and Off-Site Bookkeeping

You can pick up a lot of good clients doing write-up services, but the real money is in on-site or remote access bookkeeping. If you're charging $25 per hour and have 5 clients that you go to, 8 hours per day, 5 days a week, you will be making $52,000 per year. I can tell you that with the contact lists that you can make from this program, you will easily be able to get 5 clients on-site. It got to the point where I was turning down work because I was so overloaded. You can hire someone to go on-site or in-home as well, pay them $10 or $15 per hour and still bill out at your rate, but clients tend to be very particular when they build a trust with you. My clients wanted no one but me to do their work. They had built such a trust in me that I was able to do wire transfers to many clients' personal and business bank accounts, and I dealt with their personal financial matters as well, along with many other trust issues that they needed handled. That type of trust doesn't come easily. You <u>need</u> to be honest, and never cheat your clients. It will always come back and get you in the end. If you don't like a client, send them to someone else, but always finish the job you started, and make sure they are taken care of during the transfer. I <u>never</u> left a client high and dry. They could always depend on me, and call me up to ask even the most stupid questions without insult. On-Site Bookkeeping would include the following services for your clients.

> Payroll   (Offer a Payroll Company)
> > Process Employee Payroll
> > Payroll Tax Payments
> > Payroll Tax Reports/Quarterly/Annually
> > Year end W-2's
> Accounts Payable
> > Bill Processing on aging
> > Bill Payment
> > Filing
> > Offer to have their bills go directly to your office (P.O. Box) so you can process them more efficiently. (This is very convenient for your client considering they don't like to sit and process their bills.)

Accounts Receivable

    Invoicing

    Collections

    Filing

    Deposits/Cash Receipts

Monthly Bank Reconciliation

Sales Tax Reports (Usually Quarterly)

Workers Compensation Reports

You can offer an Off-Site Bookkeeping service as well. In this instance, you would pick up all of your clients' data and prepare the checks, invoices, and vendor bills at your office. You would then re-deliver the checks that you wrote and the invoices that you generated, so that your client could review them and send them out. If your client has you mail out payments and invoices, make sure you tell them your fee does not cover postage. It adds up quickly and you will start losing money and not making money. If your client is signed up with online banking, you could process the bill payments and have your client log in to their accounting via remote access and send the payments themselves. That way they know what you're paying. This service does take a great deal of trust between you and your client because they no longer have control of their bookkeeping. Make sure you always show them how much money they have, what checks you wrote and who you billed each week. You do this by running a checkbook register, invoice register and vendor payables due. Supply these reports to your client every time you do any of these services. You would file all of your client's records at your office and at the end of the year, give your clients their year end accounting files.

Remote Access from QuickBooks Pro® now has the capability for remote access without having to use the extremely slow software that is available in the stores today. To have remote access from your office to your client's office you <u>must</u> be operating under the same version of QuickBooks Pro®. The Premier accountant version is the same (able to talk to the Premier QuickBooks Pro® version) that your clients will use, but they both must be Premier for it to work. The remote access service is free for one year from Intuit® via website access. My computer system is integrated on a network and I have four other workstations in my office. To test the remote accesses capabilities which most of my clients are asking for, I was concerned about tying up the client's computer so I could work. That is initially what will happen. It isn't a big ordeal if they don't have a lot of activity or work to do on their computer. You can designate a time on a specific day of the week or month to have complete remote access to their computer. However if the client has a network system and is constantly billing customers, this causes a problem. Solution! I tested the system with my server and one other workstation, which has the complete 5-user package on it. I obtained access to my administrative computer from my computer, pretending that the administrator computer was the client's computer. I took over control of his computer, preformed work as usual, then went to my server and third work station and preformed other accounting functions, and recorded the transactions, and within a matter of seconds, you could view the transactions on the accountant and administrative (client) computer. QuickBooks® was able to allow the network users not to be affected by my accessing a <u>particular workstation</u> at a client's office! It's unbelievable how much travel time this saves! This is definitely the wave of the future in client services. You can perform full-charge bookkeeping from <u>your</u> office, yet work on their computer. It allows you to perform so many different accounting functions. I think this program is the perfect tool when you have your client's Accounts Payable invoices forwarded to your business. You can input all of the vendor bills, as well as pay the bills, and show your client up-to-date account information on what their payables and receivables are. It gives them a constant awareness of where their financial position is.

✓ **Other Services**

Financial Packages for Banks and Lending Institutions are also a good service to provide. Depending on the bank, sometimes they will require a CPA to "Audit" the financial reports. This is very expensive for the small business owner, so most banks will accept prepared financial reports and loan applications from the company's bookkeeper. Don't let them intimidate you if you don't have the piece of paper stating that you are a CPA. It wouldn't be any different than the small business owner printing out his or her own financial reports from QuickBooks® and giving it to the bank. The difference in you doing it is that you are a professional and you can assist in filling out the paperwork and making sure that the balance sheet isn't wrong. You can also answer questions from the bank a lot more fluently than the small business owner can, because you prepared it. A lot of companies trying to get SBA Loans need help, especially with a Cash Flow Projection (a business financial plan). The Cash Flow Projection included with this book is what I have created and use for my clients in submitting loan packages when the bank requests a "look into the future."

Audit <u>Preparation</u> can send a lot of money your way. If your client is being audited for a prior year and they never had a handle on their accounting, chances are the IRS Auditor is not going to allow expenses that were completely justifiable if they are looking through a box of receipts. You can come in and put the box into a story for your client. That story would tell the IRS Agent what the business did, with back-up documentation to prove it, and would not make the business owner look so bad.

Bookkeeping Training and Consulting is the best way for you to "teach" your clients the correct way to do their bookkeeping, all the way down to filing. If you become a QuickBooks Pro® Advisor, you will get a lot of requests from clients to help train their on-site bookkeeper as well as the owner. If you offer consulting in that scenario as well, this would be a good opportunity for you to go in and review the current structure of the businesses bookkeeping system, and to advise your client on the best solution to make their system work better. Show them what they are lacking and where they can better themselves, write up a streamlined procedure system, and provide it to them in a three-ring binder.

Tax Preparation (If licensed) is another good source of revenue, but please read my advice and suggestions in Chapter 7. That will give you a better understanding of what to expect.

QuickBooks® setup and installation is a good way to land a monthly client. Normally the client is just looking for help setting up their QuickBooks® software the correct way, but by the time you're done, they feel overwhelmed with the amount of work it's going to take to keep it current and up to date. Since you were the one who installed it, they will be calling you first.

I was asked if I was going to write a book on how to do Fraud and Financial Crimes. That will have to be another book. Anyone, even a bookkeeper, can "investigate" the client's books to see if someone is stealing money. But to become a Certified Fraud Examiner or a Certified Forensic Accountant does take a lot of experience, and a degree in accounting if you don't have the equivalent in experience (which is 10 years of accounting, along with a number of reference letters from clients and colleges stating that you are honest and hold a great deal of integrity). The test is harder than the CPA Exam because not only do you have accounting laws, rules and standards, you also have to learn the system of investigating, interviewing, and report presentation. If you have the investigative bug and meet the criteria, the Association of Certified Fraud Examiners is a national organization that you can join as a member. Once approved as a member you can sit to take the exam. To date there are approximately 20,000 CFE's in the United States, most of them are CPAs as well. Some are in the FBI, and some are just accountants like me who want to do more. You can charge five times as much per hour when you are a CFE, and have more variety in your services!

Organizational skills are the key! As an important part of your service, you must supply your clients with the proper organizational tools to keep proper accounting records. If you show the client the correct way from the beginning, it won't be so difficult to teach them to maintain their records correctly. The most efficient way to keep accounting records is in an annual binder. You must always segregate each fiscal year for accounting and tax purposes. Depending on the size of the business you are doing the books for, a 2½-inch binder works the best. Separate each month by using dividers. You can purchase the dividers that come with Jan–Dec printed on the tabs (they're obviously more expensive, but look more professional), or you can purchase the yellow dividers with the white tabs that you write on. There are two separate ways of organizing financial information. The way I prepare and submit financial reports to my clients is with a Vello Binding Machine. The covers are very professional looking and hold the clients' monthly financial reports. The machine costs around $100 and the report covers and plastic combs run about $25 for a box of 25, but it looks clean and professional. The 3-ring binders are best used for clients that you do weekly accounting for. You want to make sure that they have a weekly Accounts Receivable Aging, Sales Report, Accounts Payable Aging and Check Register printed from QuickBooks® or what ever accounting software they are using. In this instance you would need four binders segregated by report type and divided by month. This is an easy, convenient way for your client to find information when you are not there, because I guarantee they will get frustrated trying to find it in QuickBooks® themselves! In the beginning of my business I used the 2½-inch binder for the finalized end of the month financial reports as well. Once I was completed with the month-end financials, I would 3-hole-punch the reports so the client could file it in their binder. After a while, I wanted to make it more presentable and professional looking so I invested in the Vello Bind Machine. The one I use can be purchased at www.quill.com. They are an online office supply store that opens a vendor account for just about everyone and their prices are pretty reasonable. Make sure that you make a duplicate copy of <u>all</u> documents that you give to your clients, and file it in your binders. That way if they ever have a question concerning a document or entry you made, you will always have everything that your client is looking at. You never want to be caught unprepared. It tends to look as if you don't know what you're doing.

✓ Pricing Structure and Going Rates

The beauty about being your own boss is that you can be selective about who you want to do work for. Don't ever let anyone sell you short. If you walk in with the confidence and know how, your rate will not matter once your client knows what you are capable of. The going rate for a <u>new</u> bookkeeping service is $25 per hour. Once you are established and have built a strong business relationship with your clients, then depending on the work that is done, the rate is between $30 and $50 per hour. You never want to charge more than $25 per hour when you are on site at a client's office, until you feel very comfortable with the situation. $40 an hour for a bookkeeper is the maximum that you will get on site. However, if you're good, you will get it. When you do monthly accounting for clients at "your" home office, depending on the size of the client, you can charge them a set fee. I actually called around to various bookkeeping services getting pricing to see what the competition was charging. It is a very common practice. You just don't let on to who you are, and they are more than willing to share their rates with you. Some of my clients that I did monthly bookkeeping for would balance out to an average of $40 to $90 per hour. Once you get the hang of the routine, you can breeze through your work. One client wrote a very large amount of checks per month and I charged a base fee of $245. They wrote approximately 120 checks per month (they used COD with vendors), and I was able to get their work done in 4 hours. Another client had little activity, maybe 20 checks per month, if that, and I charged a "minimum fee" of $100 per month. It took me an hour and a half to do their work. I made about $90 per hour from that client. My set fees did include year-end processing, but now that I look back, I should have charged an additional fee because of the amount of time it takes to close out books. I didn't have any hidden charges that they weren't aware of. If you choose to charge your clients to prepare year-end reports, you need to inform them of those charges in your commitment letter. That way they will have proof of your charges, and will not be surprised when they get your bill. My suggestion is to charge a flat on-site rate of $25 per hour, and $35 per hour on month-end or weekly bookkeeping done at your office. You just need to estimate how long it takes you to do their work when you're submitting a bid. If you estimate that a client writes about 50 checks per month and has 5 employees (with a payroll service), it should take you about 4 hours to complete all of the work, including reconciling bank accounts, the A/R accounts, A/P accounts, and the payroll registers from the service. You would then submit a proposal with all of the services you provide at the rate of $35 per hour with an average of 4 hours per month.

The general fee for setting up accounting when you first get an account is based upon an hourly rate. You should charge your hourly fee, and give the client an estimated amount of time it will take you to put everything together. If you feel it will take you longer than your client is really willing to pay, estimate a setup fee that is in their ballpark. You want to land the account, and if you keep a client happy, you will make more money from them in the long run by giving them a "deal" to begin services. Generally you would only go back to the beginning of a current fiscal year unless they are involved in an audit, in which case you would charge your hourly rate for the entire amount of time it took you to prepare everything. The different breakdown can give you a more general idea of what you should charge.

If transferring client data from a different bookkeeping service, you wouldn't go back and re-enter all of the prior data because they should already have that information. You would post your entries to create a balance sheet matching the last month-end balance sheet you received, along with the income and expenses. (This information is listed in your instruction portion of this manual.) It shouldn't take you longer than an hour to prepare this information in your system, and frankly, I have yet to find a client who felt they should pay you to re-enter this data. **Do not charge them!** Who should tell the old accountant or bookkeeper that they're fired? The client should! The old accountant or bookkeeper deserves the consideration of an explanation as to why their services were terminated. If it were you, wouldn't you want to know? If your client doesn't have the gumption or nerve to handle this uncomfortable task, suggest they write a letter. It is an easy way out, but letters do seem to avoid any verbal confrontation unless the recipient gets upset. Everyone has the right to an explanation, even if it's just a matter of a change of pace.

If beginning your books from scratch, **charge them for this!** They are providing you with all of their receipts and records to become more organized with their accounting. This is your service to them, and they do not have any pre-existing reports for you to go from. Estimate according to the number of months you have to enter the data from, and charge them accordingly. If it is November, and they were in business since January, this is obviously going to take you a considerable amount of time to post and double-check their books. Let them know it is time consuming, and bill them for your time. If this client's work could generally take you 4 hours per month to prepare, you can inform them in a proposal that it will take you approximately 50 hours to compile all of their data. If they think it is too much, show them the breakdown. $35 per hour on a monthly bookkeeping service is $140 per month. If you're completing all of their current year accounting, they would have paid you $1,540 from January to November anyway. You can also progressively bill them for your time. Every week, bill them 12 hours ($420) so they don't have to pay one big lump sum. Estimate your time preparation based upon this assumption, even if your client has only 2 months to set up. You can give them a proposal that would estimate your time at 5 hours for $175, then a monthly fee of $140 for monthly bookkeeping. If you go to their office to prepare all of the accounting, bill them for your time there. If it takes you three trips of 8 hours each time, bill them for all of it. Always remember that you want to make your client happy, yet you don't want to sell yourself short. Use your best judgment on what you feel comfortable with. It is your company, you need to provide a professional and convenient service for your clients, but you also must remember that you are the boss. Your clients will build respect and trust with you, and I have yet to find a client who ever made me feel like I was beneath them. Unfortunately I can tell you that each one of my employers always reminded me of that in one way or another.

Bookkeeping Training and Consulting: I recommend that you charge an hourly rate for this service. If you start out and your rate is $25 per hour, that is what you charge your clients. Current QuickBooks® Advisors cost on average $50 per hour for QuickBooks® training. My suggestion is that if you are currently charging $25 per hour for bookkeeping, add another $10 to your hourly fee for QuickBooks® training and consulting. Once you are more widely known and requested, bump it up to $50 to be more competitive with other advisors.

QuickBooks® Install and Set-Up: Charge your QuickBooks® Training and Consulting hourly rate with a minimum number of hours. My minimum time is 4 hours. If it takes less then 4 hours, you still get your minimum hours, so you would charge your client $35 x 4 hours = $140. If you go over the 4-hour minimum, charge them your total hours. If your time gets a bit out of hand on the hours, let your client know when it goes over an offensive budget number, so they are not surprised when they get your bill. You can always negotiate a discount. It's better to make sure they can pay you an acceptable fee, rather than being stuck with an un-collectable invoice and an angry client.

Audit Preparation: Charge your hourly fee. If the Audit is a long drawn-out task, your client may want to negotiate a set fee, so make sure you get your money's worth.

Bank Financial Packages: Charge a set fee for this service. A reasonable fee to charge for Financial Packages if you're a bookkeeping service would be $175; this would cover you up to seven hours at $25 per hour to prepare and fill out the forms, along with the endless phone calls the bank is going to give you. If it's preparing the financials from a box of receipts, charge by the hour! For Financial Business Plans (the cash flow projection), I charge a minimum of 4 hours, plus an hourly rate. In this instance, you have to investigate numbers, costs and payroll information in association with the business type. It is a time-consuming job.

Billing by Piecework: A lot of new bookkeeping services bill by piecework. Piecework is when you charge per transaction. If your client has you entering Accounts Payable Bills, cutting checks, and Invoicing, they charge by the piece of paper that you input. From my research, rates can vary from .30 cents per piece and up. I can tell you many reasons why I don't agree with this system. Clients call with questions all the time. At times they have you on the phone for an hour and get upset if you try to bill them for it. If you bill by piecework you can't charge for a piece of phone call. Piecework is pennies, and in order to be competitive, you need to have a low piecework rate, in which case you can never recover the time you spend talking to clients. When you bill by the hour, you can increase your billings to moderately accommodate the time it took you to prepare the work.

It is also very common to have two different hourly rates: one rate for on-site services and one rate for off-site services. This will cover your travel time because your client won't like you to charge them for this. The standard price break per hour between on-site and off-site work is $5 per hour. So if you go to your client's office to do their bookkeeping, instead of charging $25 per hour, charge $30 per hour. Your gas and travel time will be covered in the markup. My suggestion is, however, in the beginning when you are just starting out, charge $25 per hour because you are new. When time progresses and your clients are more comfortable and you start receiving a lot of referrals, then make the split rate available for the new referrals and gradually increase your rate with your current clients. When increasing your rates with current clients, do it in small steps because they might get sticker shock. You can do it in $2.50 increments instead of one big jump. If you are good and they really like your work, they will pay for it.

Smaller Town Rates: If you live in Stump Jump, USA, you are most likely going to have to travel to the closest bigger city or town to get good bookkeeping work. If that's not an option and you live in a small town that doesn't have a great deal of cash to throw around, your rate is going to be less per hour. The best way to find what your competitive rate will be is to call a temp agency and get a quote for a full-charge bookkeeper. Don't tell them you are trying to find out what the going rate is. Tell them you might need to hire a bookkeeper and you need a quote. See what their bid comes in at and go by that number to be competitive. As I mentioned before, a bookkeeping service is really no different than a temp service. An employer will pay for a contracted rate from a temp agency rather than paying to have a full-time employee. The only difference is, the employee thinks they have to settle for $10 per hour, when a professional service or temp agency doesn't have to settle.

Billing for Direct Expenses: If you intend on billing your clients for direct expenses such as postage, UPS or FedEx charges, long distance charges, or even supplies, if you pay for these, make absolutely sure you let your clients know. A lawyer and CPA can get away with charging for photocopies, twenty-second telephone calls and breathing, but you can't. Your price for these items should be part of your rate, because you have much less overhead to fork out. You will offend a client if you charge them for menial expenses, so be careful and don't get greedy.

Getting Paid on your Invoices: My invoices are due Net-10 which realistically means that my clients have 10 days to pay me. After 30 days they are considered past due. I use to drop financials COD to all my clients, but I have learned that there is a trust issue with clients over an invoice. If you don't give them terms to pay your bill, then you are telling them that you don't trust them. Well, as a matter of fact that is true; you don't know them yet. The easiest way to assure that your invoices get paid on time is if you also handle your clients Accounts Payable; however, you won't always process all clients' Accounts Payable. It is very uncomfortable to sit there and wait for your client to write you a check. It makes you feel like you're so hard up for money that you get embarrassed more than anything. Asking for your money shouldn't be so intimidating, so this is what I suggest. Let your client know that your first few invoices are COD when writing your proposal, then after a few months you will invoice them at 10 days. If they start paying you too late for your schedule, put it back on a COD basis. If you have a client that has cash flow issues, stay on a COD basis. If they get really far behind, don't prepare any bookkeeping work until they catch up with their payments.

How many clients are too many to handle? I've been lucky enough to sell my books all the way to China and Australia, and an accountant from Australia had a very good question and concern. He calculated how many bookkeeping clients he would need to fill his workload based on an assumption of 4-6 hours per month per client. Only taking 4-6 hours per month servicing one client, he would need 15-20 clients to make a decent living. For write-up services, that would be an accurate assumption. It is very daunting to have 15-20 clients to service. At my peak before I changed direction and started concentrating on Fraud, I had 12 consistent clients that kept me very busy. You need a very good memory because at the drop of a hat, you need to know everything about each one of them, and if you are caught off guard, you look bad. I seem to have a very good memory. I was preparing a financial investigation for a bankruptcy client. This client had many other companies and one just wasn't cutting the mustard. The judge had the original accountant who was reviewing the financials and putting the reports together fired because they thought he was too young and too inexperienced. He was 32. I was then hired to fix what he did and put it together for the courts to understand and accept. The attorney for the client contacted me over a month after I had finalized all of the reports. I was in my car, with no documentation whatsoever to look at, and he started throwing questions at me. I could name off every last dime this client had in each bank account, who was to receive what settlement, and each line item on their balance sheet. All the while I'm on my way to the next client's office. The judge was shocked when he learned I was only 30 at the time. It's all in the presentation. The 12 clients I had brought me about $70,000 per year in income; however, 4-6 hours per week or bi-weekly was the norm, not per 4-6 per month. Most of your off-site clients will be serviced twice per month, so your billing time is really 10-12 hours per month for one client rather than 4-6. Think of it this way: your bills are generally due the 15th and the 30th of the month, and so are theirs. If you are performing their bookkeeping, they need you more than one time per month or it will be a mess. But how do you justify to your client that you are worth $480 per month when they can hire someone else? Employees are baggage. Just as I explained in Chapter 2, the difference in the cost savings of a professional rather than an employee will outweigh whatever concern your client may have about your monthly bill. So now you look at the 15-20 clients and realize it's really only 8-12 because they will normally need you more than once per month. If you get any busier than that, hire another independent bookkeeper that you oversee, pay them $20 per hour, you still charge $25 per hour, and you're making money on money. Make sure you get a good confidentiality and non-compete clause signed so the clients are still yours. The client pays your billings and your independent bookkeeper bills you.

Another good question was how to operate a bookkeeping service while still working full-time. You have to start somewhere and sometimes that is starting out part-time. What if you don't have any additional sources of income and not enough cash flow to carry you through until you start earning money? Many of us didn't quit our day job first. The way I started out part-time was to make myself available to clients on weekends and evenings. Some clients did not like this and would go with other accountants and bookkeepers who are available during regular business hours, but other clients prefer you not to interrupt their regular business hours. It doesn't matter if you do their work off site at your office or if you come into their office on the weekend or evening. When you do their work at your home office, it allows you to work at night or on the weekends while you are not at your day job. In times past, a bookkeeper was only seen at nighttime with a glowing candle and a pencil. When I first opened my service, I started out with three clients while still working full-time. I went to one client's office at 6:00 p.m. and worked until about 8:30. I did this twice per week. With the other two clients, I would pick up their files on my way home from work, or on the weekends if they were in, and work on them at my office at night or on the weekend. I had voice mail and checked my messages regularly. At that time, cell phones were not handed out like candy, so I did the unspeakable, and checked my voice mail messages at work. Now with all of the integrated spy systems, I do not recommend this. Use your own cell phone, and return phone calls on your lunch break or regular breaks so you can catch the client during business hours. I never told them that I was still working full-time for someone else. I always said that I was at a "client's" office. I met with my networking resources in the morning, at lunchtime, or in the evenings. Keep in mind, I was able to do all of this before I had children. Now as a mother, with getting kids ready for school, it is much more difficult to have so much time available before and after work. But it can be done. By the time my first daughter was born, I was 100% self-employed. It was about six months from the time I opened my business to the time I quit my job. It gave me the freedom to juggle daycare and appointments. A lot of home-based business ideas try to promote the fact that you can do it with ease while having children at home without having daycare. It isn't as easy as that. Children require high maintenance, and if you are a parent, it is a lot higher. There are constant interruptions, sibling rivalries, and demands ("Mommy, come watch this!"). Your most productive time will be when they are taking a nap, or at nighttime when they go to bed. If you can find even part-time daycare, it will help you be more productive and you will still be able to spend a lot of extra time with your children, rather than feeling overwhelmed because you can't get anything done.

Remember that your service is what is going to sell you. You have to show your clients that you are more valuable then the other bookkeeping services out there. Your work is more detailed and organized, and they are definitely getting the quality for the price. You have to list what you anticipate doing to show your potential clients and current clients the *who*, *what*, *when*, and *how* answers that they will ask you. Who is your competition? How are you better than they are? What can you provide me that they can't? When can I expect the information that I require? You must always inform each potential client of your answers even before they ask. You must <u>tell</u> them what you can do for them to make their business run more profitably; show them where they're losing money, why they're paying too much for supplies, insurance, taxes, etc. You have to be the resource that they have been looking for to help answer the questions that they don't know. Everyone seems to take accounting in college; but 90% of the students won't remember it because they found it boring and so had a complete lack of interest. Unfortunately they need that information to run a successful business, and that is where you come in!

Make sure you prepare an introduction letter to your potential client including the services that you offer and your monthly or hourly rate. (You will find a format letter in your Forms portion of this book.) It is important always to have everything in writing, for your protection as well as theirs. If they accept your proposal, make sure you complete the contract. I have noticed that a lot of bookkeepers are afraid to submit the contract to the client because there is always a sense of, "Will the client get upset?" They might, and some don't even want to sign it at all. If you are comfortable with not submitting a contract with your client, just have them sign the proposal. It is still an acceptance and authorization that they want your services. Just make sure you make two copies of the proposal and have them sign both.

Chapter 4
Step-By-Step Instructions

✓ **Setting up a Balance Sheet**

The first rule in setting up a proper balance sheet is to familiarize yourself with a Chart of Accounts. Your chart of accounts consists of all of your asset accounts such as bank, cash, receivable, fixed assets, notes receivable. Your liability accounts, accounts payable, loans, and payroll taxes. Your equity accounts such as capital contributions, distributions, and net profit. Your income accounts, and of course your expense accounts. There is a copy of my standard Chart of Accounts on pages 188-190.

General accounting firms and bookkeeping services use a numbered chart of accounts. I have included a "sample" company printed from on a QuickBooks Pro® dummy data file for you to use as a guide and example. The best and correct way to set up your chart of accounts is to make sure you always group them in the correct order. The numbering system varies for every CPA firm or bookkeeping service. There are no "correct" numbers to use. The numbering system I have set up is easy to follow and memorize. As you set up more and more companies, you'll be able to do it with your eyes closed. QuickBooks Pro® has its own set of "chart of account numbers." I always use my format because my numbering system works better for me.

Make sure your clients give you all of the necessary data to set up your balance sheet. Use your information guide on your client as you are creating their books. Are they a corporation, and if so, what type – S, C, LLC, or Sole Proprietor? Do they operate on a cash or accrual basis? Do they accumulate their receivables for invoicing and bill payment? There are key questions that you must answer while creating your client's set of books. Does your client already have an existing set of books? How do you create a duplicate set of books starting where the last bookkeeper left off? Nine out of ten times, if you take over the bookkeeping from another service, they will not give you their computer data unless you buy it from them. The best way to handle this situation is to make sure they give you their hard copies. The client is entitled to receive all hard copies back from the original preparer.

First review the financial reports (Balance Sheet, Profit and Loss, and Aging Reports) supplied from the previous bookkeeper. Do you have a current Year to Date report? That would be the ideal report to use to create your new set of books. If you do not have a YTD, you need to take all of the monthly Profit and Loss reports and total them by month. The best way to do this is on a spreadsheet. Lotus or Excel are the best software to use. Once you have created a spreadsheet with the appropriate income and expense accounts, you can segregate your columns by month and start re-entering the data. Make sure you include a final column for Year to Date totals. Once each month is entered in, make sure your totals match the previous reports; if they do, then you can take the YTD Totals from your spreadsheet report, and use that for your journal entry steps. If the client uses the accrual method for Accounts Receivable and Payable, you have to re-post each invoice accordingly. If these are on a cash basis, then you just need to make sure your income and expense accounts total out the same.

The Balance Sheet from the previous bookkeeper should not have to be re-created. A Balance Sheet will always calculate the Assets and Liabilities as of the report date. If your new set of books starts on May 1st, then take the report from the previous bookkeeper for April 30th and create a posting journal entry to record all of the financial data. (I have included a sample of how to recreate an existing set of books from the QuickBooks Pro® dummy data file.) Make sure after you make all of your journal entries that you run a report for (April 30th) to make sure your totals match the previous bookkeeper's report totals. If they do, you are now ready to continue. Unless of course the prior bookkeeper's numbers and reports were incorrect and messy – then you need to start from scratch with your own numbers based upon all data supplied.

If you are creating a set of books for a new company, you need to follow your guidelines on the information requested from the client. Do they have any SBA Loans? Where did the capital come from? Do they have miscellaneous receipts showing that they spent their personal capital on business expenses? If so, where do you apply them? On a Balance Sheet for a Sole Proprietor, you create an equity account called Owner Draw. This account needs to have two sub-accounts. A sub-account is an account associated to one particular account, but is of a different class. On the Owner Draw, the sub accounts are generally tax deductible. A sole proprietor cannot write off medical expenses or 50% Self-Employment Tax and estimated tax payments through his business; he has to do it on his 1040 tax return; so this expense would be considered an Owner Cash Advance, so to speak. It would accumulate under the owner's draw rather than under medical expenses because it is not a legitimate business expense; so we don't have to go back at the end of the year and add up all of the tax-deductible expenses. The other sub-account would be Cash Payouts to the owner in lieu of a salary. Sole Proprietors don't "take" a salary because they are already responsible for the Federal and State Taxes on their personal tax return. Whatever the Net Profit of the company is, regardless of how much Owner Draw they take, is the owner's taxable revenue.

If the company is a corporation, then generally the "Shareholder" receives a salary. If they are not on the payroll, then you must set up an Equity Account called "Distribution to Shareholder." If there were more than one shareholder, your sub-accounts under the Distribution would list each owner's name. Likewise if it is just one owner. There are limitations on what the IRS will allow for salaries and justifiable distributions to a shareholder. Make sure, if you get to this area of questioning, to ask a CPA because you don't want your client to get penalized for payroll tax evasion.

There are common questions you need to get used to asking your clients when you are picking up a new account. I have included a checklist form in the back of this book so you don't forget. Use your common judgment on how far back you need to obtain the following data. If you are picking up an account in March, and they opened in January, obviously you would need all of the following records for the past three months.

Prior Year's Tax Return (if they're an existing company)

Checkbook Register

Bank Statements

Cancelled Checks

Deposit Slips

Copies of Customer Payments (hopefully they did it)

A/P Invoices

A/R Invoices

If existing – Current Balance Sheet

If existing – Current Profit and Loss Statement

Federal Tax Identification number

State Tax ID Number

Cash Receipts they incurred for the business

Petty Cash Receipts and balance

If they own a car and it is business related, you need a copy of the car purchase note to depreciate

Equipment Purchased – all receipts

Loans (business)

Credit Card Statements (business related)

✓ **Setting up a new client**

If you pick up a new account at the beginning of a Fiscal Year, it is <u>always</u> best to enter the data directly from the checkbook register without plugging in a journal entry to make the Profit and Loss balance. If it is only a few months, it won't take you that long, and in the long run, it will be more convenient for you to research transactions that occurred, instead of only being able to review the figures in a journal entry. If your client will be using an Accounts Payable system, it won't affect the initial transactions if posted from the checking account. Just make sure you post all of the <u>current</u> A/P that are still due. I guarantee that at the end of the year when you're processing 1099's and can't run an accurate 1099's transaction report for vendors, you'll wish you had entered them in directly.

✓ **Company Fiscal Years**

Each company is created differently, yet the accounting principle is still the same. A Fiscal Year is the accounting year in which the company records its revenues and expenses. Most companies use a calendar year of January to December. When you get into bigger corporations, depending on the incorporation date, their fiscal year could be from October to September, or August to July. It is still in 12-month increments, but the calendar for earnings is recorded differently. Thus their company tax return is filed at a different time of year than what the general public is accustomed to – April 15th for individuals and Schedule C Returns (Sole Proprietors). The tax deadline date for corporations, depending on what fiscal year they are using, is March 15th, or three months after their fiscal year end.

Accounting is also separated by quarters. It is usually used for financial institutions and tax agencies for receiving their financial reports or tax reports and payments. The quarters are separated as follows:

1. Jan-Mar is your First Quarter

2. Apr-June is your Second Quarter

3. July-Sept is your Third Quarter

4. Oct-Dec is your Fourth Quarter

Always remember those quarters if you don't already know them! Payroll Tax reports, Estimated Tax payments, Sales Tax payments, and Financial Packages are always due by the last day of the following month preceding the end of a quarter.

Example: Payroll Tax 941 1st Quarter is Jan-Mar 31st and is due by April 30th. Your estimated tax payments are due the 15th day of the month preceding the end of a quarter. Sales tax reports and payments are due quarterly depending on the amount of collectable sales tax in your state. If your client processes a large taxable sale each month, then the state sales tax agency will require a monthly tax deposit along with the quarterly tax filing.

✓ Double Entry Bookkeeping

Double entry bookkeeping is not as difficult as people make it out to be. If you have never taken an accounting course and are not familiar with Debits and Credits, there is a simple rule that will help you understand what you are posting. Your checking account consists of deposits and checks/transactions that you paid. If you were keeping track of your personal finances to see how much money you spent, how would you calculate it? Every time you wrote a check, where did it go? Let's say you wrote a check for $1,000 to your mortgage lender. Your checking account would be reduced by $1,000. When you <u>reduce</u> an asset account, you are creating a "credit" (negative) transaction. The flip side to this is double entry bookkeeping. If you are reducing your checking account by $1,000 yet you want to keep track of how much it is costing you per year for your mortgage, you are going to <u>increase</u> your mortgage expense account; you are then creating a double entry to your books, which is the "debit" (addition). You add to your mortgage expense account each month that you pay it, so it is going to keep going up. Each time you write a check from your checking account it is going to go down. Just think of credit as <u>reducing</u> and debit as <u>increasing</u>.

If you make a deposit into your checking account, you are <u>increasing</u> it (debit); you then <u>reduce</u> your accounts receivable by the amount paid because you are no longer owed the money; your credit would be applied to that account. (QuickBooks Pro® automatically enters the debits and credits when writing checks or making deposits; however, you need to be able to create a journal entry and know the difference for yourself.)

71

You have probably heard the question, "When is a Debit a Credit, and a Credit a Debit"? Those entries are usually only in your equity accounts, and the CPA whom you have preparing the business returns will generally make those journal entries. If you do have to post entries to equity accounts, in QuickBooks Pro®, you will be able to see what entries just don't look right on your balance sheet. You will know if you have made an incorrect entry just by looking at the balance sheet. If you know that an Equity Account has Capital Contributions (meaning money the owner put into the company) as a negative number and their distributions are a positive number, then you did it backwards. If you took money as a draw from the company and needed to track it in your equity account, the credit entry would come out of your checking account and your debit entry would go into your equity draw account. Just make sure, if you are not a CPA and have a CPA preparing your client's tax returns, especially if the client is a corporation, that you don't make any adjustments to equity accounts without showing the CPA a copy of the journal entry. There is nothing worse than trying to complete a Corporate Tax Return when your prior year balance sheet from QuickBooks® doesn't match the Corporate Tax Returns balance sheet.

✓ **Entering Data from a Checkbook Register**

This process is very similar to entering accounts payable except you are avoiding that step of bill payment entirely. There are two reasons why you would be entering in data directly from the checkbook register. Number one, your client is set up on your monthly accounting service, and number two, you need to post checks and transactions that your client wrote while you were not at their office. It is very important that you record all new transactions that your client has created so their checkbook is always in perfect balance.

If you are entering data for the "monthly" service, you just enter it in as you would record any other check, deposit or other banking transactions. Once you have entered in all of the data, compare your balance to the one in the hard register and verify that they match. Your next step would be to reconcile the bank account from the bank statement, if you're doing a monthly service. If there are additional transactions on the bank statement that you don't show on your register, verify what they are, then post them accordingly. You always want your client's checking account to balance out to the last penny.

If you are posting transactions when you come in on a weekly basis to your client's office, make sure that is your first activity for the day. You always need to know how much money your client has to pay their bills. Once all the transactions are entered, you can work on the rest of your daily activity. Make sure that you double-check the balances and verify that they are identical. Always let the client know if there are discrepancies from a physical handwritten checkbook versus your QuickBooks® Register. Nine out of ten times when the client's balance in their checking account differs from what you show in your system, your system is the correct balance, which means you have to tell them they didn't have as much money as they thought. No one ever likes that, so when you are telling your client, make sure you know why. Is it because they went to Home Depot one too many times? Just have the backup receipt or check copy that may have not been entered so that you can explain to them with a guaranteed reason why.

✓ **Accounts Payable**

Processing invoices for payment is rather easy. It's the same thing basically as paying bills at home. QuickBooks Pro® makes this function very easy. Depending on what type of Accounts Payable service your client has you handling, it shouldn't be that big of a difference.

Most accounts are on a Net-30 day cycle except for credit cards, phone bills, and electric bills. Make sure you're posting the correct bill to the correct expense account. Luckily with accounting, you have more than one opportunity to check your entries. That is why we run end-of-the-month General Ledgers!! Familiarize yourself with the type of industry your client is in. If the client is a bar, then obviously the majority of the purchases will be alcohol. That is a Cost of Goods; it is directly related to the business product itself. You will have so many different types of clients, but once you become accustomed to their business it will be very easy to differentiate between them. The best way to make sure bills are not paid late is to cut the check a week in advance. Accounts Payable departments usually run on a semi-monthly payment cycle. Which means, they cut checks 2 times per month. Usually on the 10th and the 25th of the month: the 10th for bills due on or around the 15th, and the 25th for bills due on or around the 1st. I recommend using the 10th and 25th. Your client may have another system; if they are eager to keep using it, see if it works, and if it is not efficient and convenient, then recommend your way.

When you pay credit card bills, always make sure you reconcile the credit card statement as if it were a bank statement! This function can be done in QuickBooks Pro®, and is very easy. You can enter the credit card payment due as a bill, and when you post it to the corresponding chart of account, it would be posted under liabilities. That way it is reducing your liabilities when you pay it, and your expense accounts were already increased from entering in all of the charges posted off of the credit card receipts or statement. Also make sure you post the finance charges as well (usually you do this entry when you are reconciling the credit card.) Credit card purchases are really an accountant's worst nightmare. The receipts are relentless, but the only way to make sure you can account for everything is to enter them in the computer. Suggest to your client to use one specific credit card for business and one for personal expenses. If they don't want to because it's too much of a hassle, think of it this way – it's more billable time for you. Make sure on credit card purchases that if they are personal, you post them to the owner draw or distribution account. Everything that you write off as an expense for your client's business needs to be a justifiable business expense. If you are not sure, ask your client what the purchase was for.

When you file Accounts Payable records, make sure you separate them by year! Always separate by year! Staple the bottom 3rd portion of the computer-generated check to the corresponding bill that you have paid, and file it in the Accounts Payable folder. I recommend Acco-Fastening the bills to the manila folder; that way they aren't loose, and don't fall out. Make sure you file in order by date, with January on the bottom, and the most current payment on top. Your client does not do your job, which is why they hired you. If they don't know where to find something, it will be extremely frustrating for them. Your job is to make their business run smoothly! It's okay to create a miscellaneous A,B,C Accounts Payable folder for vendors rarely used, but it is always more convenient to make a folder for each vendor you are using. If your client was ever involved in an IRS Audit, it will run more smoothly by having the hard copies of invoices, checks and receipts in order!

If you are not using computer-generated checks, and are writing them by hand (or your client writes the checks), you will post the checks from the client's register to your computer bank register. Always make sure each manual bank register has an exact end balance after you enter in any transactions. If the handwritten checks don't have check stubs with them, then I suggest having your client invest in a date/check stamp. Stamp the invoice with the payment date, check number, and check amount, and file it in the corresponding Accounts Payable file.

One of the most beneficial aspects of doing your client's Accounts Payable is that you're in charge of paying the bills. Thus you always make sure your invoice is paid on time. It is a great leverage to keep your invoices from going past due.

Once per month you need to audit the Accounts Payable due file. The best time to do this is when the vendor statements come in the mail. Go through all of the open vendor bills and mark them off of your current Accounts Payable Report. Use the detail bills by vendor report from QuickBooks® so that it shows each invoice that is due along with the invoice number and due date. That way you won't be surprised if there was a vendor bill that was missed or not entered in the system.

✓ Accounts Receivable

If you offer Accounts Receivable, make sure you get your client's billing out as soon as possible. If they don't get their bills out, they won't get paid. Also make sure you are invoicing correctly. If you're not sure about something, pull a prior invoice to see how it was done. That is the best way to learn without feeling stupid for asking.

Make sure you post the income to the correct account. It is important for budget purposes to keep track of the receivables. Each time you invoice, QuickBooks Pro® automatically posts the double entry bookkeeping to your balance sheet account (Accounts Receivable). The way to reduce your balance against your Accounts Receivable is to receive a payment or create a credit memo.

If you are making a cash receipt, QuickBooks Pro® can also do that. It is the same function as entering in an invoice, yet QuickBooks Pro® will automatically apply the cash sale to your income account rather than your balance sheet account (Accounts Receivable). A cash sale means receiving payment immediately for services or goods. It would also be directly deposited to your checking, petty cash or Waiting to be Deposited account in QuickBooks®.

Deposits, whether in actual cash or checks, are very important to keep track of. The number one mistake small businesses make is not to make a photocopy of the checks that they deposit into their business or personal bank account – especially if it is an Owner Contribution Check. It is very frustrating trying to post customer payments from a bank deposit slip when you have no idea who paid them or for what invoice! A copy of the check in question automatically solves that problem. If your client is in charge of making the deposits, do whatever it takes to make them copy their checks – even if they have to use their fax machine or scan them in! I can't tell you how important it is to prove where the money that they are depositing to their bank account came from! No one wants to pay income tax on a deposit that they made as a loan to the company, yet they don't have backup documentation to prove where it came from. That is exactly what will happen. Each check copy should be stapled to a copy of the deposit slip, and added together they should equal the total deposit for that day. If your client does not have a duplicate deposit summary, print out the deposit summary in QuickBooks® after you have received all customer payments, and go to the next step of depositing them to the QuickBooks® bank account. You can print the screen before you close and record the transaction. Just remember that an accountant's and bookkeeper's job is to justify and prove that what they are creating on paper has backup documentation for everything they post. It is a thinker's game. If you have a deposit, think of everything the IRS will try to do to disprove your claim. Your only defense is to make an excellent paper trail, and you will win the game. File the copies of the deposit slips and checks in a folder named Xyz Company Deposits, Year 200x. File from January to December, and of course start the new year with a new deposit folder. Make sure that when each month is finished, your attached copies of checks and bank deposit slips have the same total as your bank statements. This is where you can double-check your work! That is why it is actually hard for an accountant/bookkeeper to make a lot of mistakes. There are so many opportunities to check your totals before you submit any reports to your clients.

If you offer a collection service on accounts receivable, I have enclosed some letters that will help you collect on past due invoices. Make sure that you are always courteous to your client's customers, and that you give them the opportunity to negotiate a payment arrangement. Even though you aren't an employee of your client, you are still representing them in that fashion. Always start by sending Accounts Receivable Statements on the last day of every month. Customers like to know how much they owe, especially if there is an inconsistent amount on their bill. If the invoice is over 35 days, you can send a friendly letter letting the customer know they are past due. After 40 days, you can call the customer, and follow up with another letter. If you get to a point where the customer is refusing to pay an invoice, always suggest to your client the small claims option. If your client is continuing to do work for the customer, tell your client to withhold any additional work until the customer makes a payment of some sort.

File your accounts receivable in the same way that you file the accounts payable. Organization is the key. If everything is convenient and easy to find, your clients will be very happy with your work. As with every other task, make sure you start each year over with new files.

Use the same process with the Accounts Payable by auditing your Accounts Receivable Customer Bills Due once per month. You want to make sure that all invoices due are accounted for and a customer doesn't owe your client money that slipped through the cracks.

✓ **Payroll**

I'll say it time and time again: you will get more business from a payroll service than doing it yourself! I'll give you four good reasons why you should not do payroll in-house.

1. A payroll service will under-bid your price by at least 40%.
2. A payroll service will bring you more business than you could make from doing payroll.
3. If you make a payroll tax error, the IRS will hold you and your client accountable. (Whoever signs the form is responsible for the accuracy of the tax report) Your client could come back to you to request you pay any penalties and interest incurred by the IRS or state.
4. It takes up too much time to be able to offer direct tax payment to the IRS. It is more convenient for the client to have this service; that way the payroll taxes and reports to the state and IRS are never late.

5. Do you really think it will be easy to take vacations and schedule around clients who need weekly payroll or even bi-weekly payroll if you are out of town even for a few days? Payroll is a very demanding service!

If, after considering these reasons, you have a client that still wants you to do their payroll, it is actually a very easy function. QuickBooks Pro® has a payroll system that works very easily. The most important thing is setting up your balance sheet correctly to account for the payroll tax liabilities that the company will incur each time a payroll is created. I listed out the correct way to set this up in your sample company on your chart of accounts. Each time you generate a payroll, QuickBooks Pro® will take your payroll liabilities from each paycheck and post it to the balance sheet accounts as long as you set them up the proper way. After each payroll is created, run your payroll reports, which would include:

1. Employee Summary
2. Payroll Tax Liability

The reports that are generated in QuickBooks Pro® often have different names. You can change the name of a report or create a custom report to fit your needs. You need to familiarize yourself with this report function. I often modify the name of a report to a more proper name.

Payroll taxes payments are due semi-monthly or monthly depending on the date that the IRS and state issued to your client. They base this number on the amount of tax liability, and if it's high they want it sooner. The IRS payment for Federal Withholding, Medicare, and Social Security is either paid by ACH debit (a convenience from payroll services) or deposited to your client's bank. The bank is then responsible for sending the IRS deposit coupon and payment directly to the IRS. Your payment of state withholding and state disability will be mailed to the correct state department, and must be postmarked on or before the date that it is due. Your client should have payroll tax coupons for both Federal and state which you use to make the payments. If they do not, call your local state tax department and the IRS to order the coupon booklets. You can also go online and order them direct from the IRS or state government website.

Your payroll tax reports are due quarterly. Make sure you make the payments on time! The penalties are ridiculous, and I'm sure your clients wouldn't be pleased paying them. Run Quarterly (three-month) payroll summary and tax liability reports at the end of each quarter. Use those reports as a basis in filling out your payroll taxes. (Make sure you didn't run a YTD report.) You are reporting each quarter individually. You will prepare a Year to Date report at the end of the calendar year along with processing the employee W2's. Make sure when you are preparing the Year End reports that you go back to each prior Quarter report and add the gross wages, payroll tax liabilities, and payroll tax payments from each report together. Those totals should equal the total you are submitting on your Year End tax returns. If the totals do not match, find the error before you submit the payroll report, otherwise it is wrong and you will be penalized. W2's are processed in January following the end of a calendar year. If your client is on a fiscal year that ends in a different month, you still have to create your payroll taxes and W2's on a calendar year basis. Even though your clients use a different accounting period, the general population files their personal tax returns on a calendar year basis. You can order W2's from the IRS, but you will have to type in the information. QuickBooks Pro® can print W2's, and it will save you a lot of time. You can purchase the forms from McBee Bookkeeping, any Office Supply Store, or even from QuickBooks Pro®. If you have made a business relationship with a representative from McBee, then they will generally give you the best discounts! Use your contacts in every way possible! You also have to purchase the forms yourself because this expense should be included in your fee to your client.

If you are using a payroll service to generate the entire payroll, they will do everything for you. All you have to do is enter in the figures when you receive the payroll reports from the service. I cannot stress this enough: you <u>need</u> to enter the payroll in as if you are creating a paycheck. A lot of bookkeeping and accounting services just make a journal entry to record the payroll at the end of the month to post to the accounts. I can assure you, there will be times when you need a Year to Date on an employee, yet you don't have all of the information from the payroll service because the month hasn't been completed yet. You need to be prepared for every situation your client needs, and if you can't print out that report with all of the details then you will look bad. It is also another tool to use to make sure the payroll service didn't make any accounting errors. If you enter in the payroll from the service as if you are creating a payroll check, your liability accounts will always be correct. You will have gross wage information on all of the employees, and your accounting will be accurate. If you just enter the payroll in as a journal entry, there is no way you could run anything on an employee to find earnings, tax payments, etc. You would have to go through the payroll reports and add up each payroll for the year to come up with a total. Wouldn't that be time-consuming and inconvenient? Think logically when you're creating books. The easy way out is not always best.

✓ Bank Reconciliation

QuickBooks Pro® reconciles bank accounts, credit card accounts, and even the A/R and A/P, which is very convenient. You must be on top of reconciling your client's bank accounts as well as their credit card accounts if necessary. Knowing how much money is accounted for is your most important job! QuickBooks® makes it so easy to reconcile, but in case you ever have to reconcile the accounts manually, then I have enclosed a bank reconciliation form for you to use. Make sure you take the bank statement and the checkbook register, and include the prior balances. The easiest way to reconcile your bank account is to take the bank statement and mark off each check and deposit that has cleared the bank. On the top portion of your reconciliation report, include the prior month's ending bank balance according to the bank statement (and your last month's reconciliation records) subtract all of the checks and automatic payments (loans) that cleared the bank, and add deposits and other credits that cleared the bank. If you have bank finance charges that weren't recorded in your checkbook register for that month but cleared the bank, you add that into the total as well. That end balance is what your <u>actual</u> balance is at the bank as of the statement date. Next you take your checkbook register balance for the end of the current month, add any checks that have <u>not</u> cleared the bank and deduct any deposits that have <u>not</u> cleared the bank. The total on the top portion of the reconciliation should match exactly with the total of the bottom reconciliation. If this does not happen, you need to find out where the error is. Staple a copy of the bank reconciliation, whether it is from QuickBooks Pro® or a manual reconciliation, and staple it to that corresponding bank statement. Create a file called Bank Statements (with the name of the bank and account number listed on the label). As with anything else, only keep one corresponding year in each folder!

✓ **Sales Tax Report**

Each State is different in preparing sales tax reports. Contact your State Tax Office, and order their Sales Tax Booklet. Study the laws and regulations governing your particular state. If your client deals with resale make sure you always get a resale number from their customers on file. You will need that number if you are ever audited, to prove that your business is reselling a product to another business for the purpose of resale, which means that there isn't a sales tax liability for that particular customer sale.

Sales tax payments are generally due quarterly unless your client has high retail sales. If that is the case, check with your State Tax Agency to find out what payment schedule your client falls under. Their tax booklet will show you step by step how to fill out a tax form. If you are not sure, call the tax agency. They have agents who can help you.

If you are charging sales tax on your client's invoices, make sure you're charging the right sales tax amount. A lot of times, each county in a particular city area will have a different tax rate. At the end of each quarter (or scheduled tax pay date) run a Sales Report to double-check your figures. Use that report to generate your sales tax return. You will take the gross sales, deduct any non-taxable portion of that sale, and thus will have your taxable gross sales. Your Sales Tax Return and your Sales Report need to match as well!

✓ Workers Compensation

Workers Compensation reports are often completed by a payroll service as an extra fee. They are generally due on a quarterly basis depending on the insurance company you are using. They are very easy to fill out, and if you're not sure on the form, you can always contact the agent to walk you through it. It is very important to make sure you have accurate payroll report totals when making a Workers Compensation report because they like to nail you for underpayment. It always makes you look better when you can save your client money. That will definitely make them happy.

At the end of the workers compensation contract period, which is in twelve-month increments, the workers compensation carrier will prepare an audit of your client's payroll records. I imagine my attitude with the insurance industry is very poor with good reason, but one of the most successful internal audits that I offer is for workers compensation. They are not done on behalf of the insurance company, obviously! It is always on behalf of my clients. Just like clockwork, at the end of a fiscal workers comp period, your client's audit will come in the mail with a nice little form attached to it showing a balance due for the year in underpayment of workers comp insurance. Most times, it's not a small balance due; and if it is small, it isn't worth any time investigating. It's normally in the thousands. At that point, I come in and investigate their numbers on what they are claiming my client's payroll was for that audit period. It really amazes me how they come up with these numbers, but they do. I investigate what their claim is, base it upon actual payroll filed with the Federal and State Government as well as the canceled checks and internal payroll registers, and break them down by category and work code. I pull their contract out showing the rate per category to make sure my basis doesn't have anything they could catch me on, and I prepare a spreadsheet and a counter-claim with actual payroll based on category, and send it over to the auditor with a letter contradicting their bill due. If their numbers are wrong and your client doesn't owe them thousands in additional workers compensation insurance, they are legally obligated to credit the balance due. Normally they will just claim ignorance or the big "oops" theory. Now I'm sure a lot of it is not intentional, just unqualified employees trying to perform a job they have only been doing for two weeks. But you can be the hero by saving your client money. Just make sure that you never promise something that you are not 100% sure about! If a situation like this occurs, the best response to your client would be, "Let me look at the numbers to see if the insurance company is right." That leaves both doors wide open in case you have to come back and say, "Yes, they were correct and you do owe the money."

✓ **Financial Reports**

I have enclosed a Monthly Check List as well as a Year End Checklist that will help you remember what reports and tasks you need to complete each month and at the end of the year.

Before you ever submit any report to your client, review it for errors and double-check your numbers!!! Make sure that your asset and liability accounts add up, as well as your Profit and Loss Reports (Income Statement). For instance, the reports you would include in a monthly financial package for your client are listed below. Make sure your entries such as checks, invoices, bills and journal entries are posted to the correct account by running a general ledger report. I would always take my A/R Aging, A/P Aging, and Profit and Loss, and make sure the totals on those reports matched what I was submitting on my balance sheet.

- Balance Sheet
- Monthly Profit and Loss Statement

- Trial Balance
- Accounts Payable Aging (Unpaid Bills Detail)
- Accounts Receivable Aging (Open Invoices)
- General Ledger
- Monthly Payroll Reports (unless they use a service)
- WIP Report (Work in Progress)
- Quarterly Profit and Loss Statement
- YTD Profit and Loss Statement

I have printed reports from the QuickBooks Pro® Sample Company. They are listed under Memorized Reports. Familiarize yourself with those reports and how the totals always correspond with each other.

Keep in mind, depending on how extensive your service is, any financial reports that you prepare are un-audited. This means that they were never verified and confirmed through an Audit by a CPA firm. If you are only providing basic bookkeeping services to your clients such as accounts payable, accounts receivable, reconciling bank accounts but not financial reporting, you can still run these financial reports for your clients. The numbers are just not finalized until you submit your information to the clients or your CPA to run finalized financial reports. A Finalized Financial Report and an Audited Financial Report are not the same thing either. Generally a company will only need Audited Financial Reports if required by a Bank, Investor, or if the company is a Publicly Traded Corporation. A Finalized Financial Report is financial information reviewed and prepared by a professional after all of the monthly data and accounting information is entered, reconciled, reviewed and finalized. These reports are acceptable by banks and lenders as well as clients. It gives a financial overview of the company's monthly, quarterly and annual activity, telling a story about how they did. If banks requested Audited Financial Reports from small business owners just for obtaining business loans and credit lines, the small business owner would never make it because these are very expensive. You figure a CPA is charging upwards of $150 per hour. To audit small business books and verify every entry, canceled check, vendor bill and customer invoice so it is accounted for and is true to its word could take hundreds of hours. So a professionally prepared financial report is quite acceptable.

✓ Audit Preparation

Preparing audits can be very financially rewarding. I was involved in a two-year audit with one of my biggest clients, and I made about $20,000. As an accountant I was not able to be present at the hearing (you are required to be a CPA or an Enrolled Agent), yet I was hired to <u>prepare</u> all of the documentation and backup paperwork for the audit itself. I was also extensively involved with the IRS Agent completing the audit. I spent many hours on telephone conferences with the owner of the corporation as well as the attorneys and the auditor. It was a very rewarding experience.

I was literally given 10 boxes of receipts, check stubs and bank statements, and a copy of two prior-year tax returns (the years being audited). There weren't any computer files, backup disks, checkbook registers or anything of importance to go by. Everything had to be recreated from the ground up. The first place I started was organizing the files by year. Once I separated the year, I hired my cousin to file them in manila folders by vendor, bank statement and receipts. I paid her $10 per hour while I charged my client $25 per hour. It took her about 14 hours to put those files together. During those 14 hours I was able to recreate a checkbook register by entering in all of the canceled checks from the bank, and reconciling the bank account. Whatever canceled check was missing was found by the bank statement, which made my job a lot easier! It took me about 320 hours to put those two years together. After I was finished, I ran my general ledger to review each account entry, check entry, and deposit made. I had to call prior vendors to get copies of the invoices we didn't have that were over $150 (the lowest amount in question) to show proof of what the expense was for. It took a lot of time researching, especially when companies changed names, were bought out or closed. My client started out owing the IRS $110,000 for the two years, and after the audit was finally over, the actual amount he ended up owing was only $19,000. This was a very successful audit. If you are ever involved in preparing audit documentation, always start at the beginning, and research, double-check records, and justify against the tax return filed to find out where the deduction came from.

One of my specialties was cleaning up books that were incompetently prepared by another accountant or bookkeeper. I used the same principle in doing this as I did in preparing the audit. You need to organize, review documentation, research, and show your client how their books should be prepared!

✓ **Financial Packages to Banking Entities**

If your client received a SBA Loan or any type of funding from a financial institution, then the Lender/Bank will require you to a prepare Quarterly as well as a Year to Date financial packages. The purpose of this is to let the lender or bank know how financially sound the company is that they lent money to. They want to make sure that their money is invested wisely, and that your client isn't suffering from a financial hardship.

The banks would like the reports by the 15th of the proceeding month, giving you approximately 15 days to complete all the accounting necessary for the previous month and quarter. You generally get your bank statements by the 4th of the month, so that gives you realistically 11 days to complete everything. The more proficient you are in supplying banks with financial data, the more inclined they are to think of you when another customer needs a bookkeeper or accountant.

The reports that you must file on a quarterly basis are:
1. Balance Sheet (as of end date of quarter)
2. Profit and Loss Statement – Quarterly
3. Profit and Loss Statement – Year to Date (ending at the quarter)
4. Trial Balance

5. Accounts Receivable Aging
6. Accounts Payable Aging
7. Work In Progress (WIP) report or Job Progress Report

After completing these reports for the bank, make sure you make a copy for your files along with your client's files. If the bank were to call and question an item on one of the reports you submitted, and you or your client didn't have it, you would feel like an idiot.

✓ **Work In Progress**

A WIP report as we actually call it is mainly for a product or project client. Let's say you have a client that is a construction company. They begin a job in January that they bid out at $50,000; it is now March, and only 70% of that job is complete. It is also the end of the 1st Quarter. We want to know how much revenue (gross and net) is still due on this job. We'll say the customer has paid a deposit of $10,000 for this job, and we had purchased all of the materials to complete this job, costing $7,500. We had two men working this job that were paid $15 per hour plus an additional 15% in payroll taxes. They have already spent 480 hours each (960 total) on the job and the job is expected to go another 288 hours each to complete this job. Our WIP report would be listed as follows:

Estimate	Payment	Bal Due	Labor	Materials	Job Costs	Net Profit	Such as sub-contracted labor
50,000	10,000	40,000	26,496	7,500	0	16,004	

The amount from the WIP report that would be entered on your balance sheet account would be $40,000. The labor and materials have already been accounted for, yet the job is not complete. Since it is a contract, and it is not billable yet because the job is not completed, the balance on the contract is still considered an asset to the company. If you did not create a WIP report for your client, their Net Profit would show a different story than there actually is. Once the job is complete, and an invoice is created for the balance due, you would create a journal entry reducing your WIP account, and increasing your income account.

Try to steer your clients towards job costing in QuickBooks®, if they are in an industry where you would need to know how much money it cost you for each job you performed. You can budget the numbers as well as progress bill; which will take away a great portion of the need to break down a WIP report. If your client creates Estimates through QuickBooks® which allows them to progress bill, the WIP report is no longer necessary. If your client does not want to track job costs in QuickBooks®, yet doesn't feel like they should pay taxes on a deposit they received in December for work that won't start until January, then the WIP report is going to be the paper trail that saves you. If there aren't any labor hours, expenses or materials purchased from the date of the deposit received to the next fiscal period, your burden of proof is realized. QuickBooks® reports can be imported to Excel, with which you can make customized spreadsheets to create more in-depth reports.

✓ **Training and Consulting**

Another form of profitable cash flow is training and consulting. A lot of companies are only interested in hiring someone to come in and train on basic accounting procedures, computer programs and organizational skills. If you land an account that only requires you to train an on-site bookkeeper, there is a very good chance that after you train your client, you can still pick up their monthly bookkeeping account. That is an ideal account to have. No only are you able to train the office assistant the "proper" way to run an accounting department, but you can fine-tune their work at the end of the month for financial reports, and year-end statements and possibly taxes as well.

Make sure you learn every possible troubleshooting situation, and absorb everything you can from this book that will help you strengthen your skills to be a strong trainer. The basic rule for training and consulting is to have patience. I don't know how many clients I have had who literally didn't understand anything about bookkeeping or accounting. You need to spell it out in layman's terms, and give them documentation to go back on. They don't know how to do it, or they wouldn't have hired you.

✓ Budgeting

Budgeting is a very important tool to become brilliant at. If you can save your client time and money, they will not only appreciate you more, they will always be able to justify your fees because you are saving them that plus more in return.

To have the proper budgeting tools, QuickBooks Pro® has set up a budget system that is very easy to use. You can import the reports to Excel and create a more accurate "Cash Flow Projection" spreadsheet; however, I am including the cash flow schedule that I created in Excel. It works perfectly, and the formulas are already there for you. This is the perfect tool to use to budget on a monthly basis. You can modify the report to fit your client's information. When updating your budgets in Excel, I suggest that you always create a new page. You can do this by selecting *edit*, *move* or *copy sheet*. Select *copy sheet* and mark the month you want to copy. Then just double-click on the bottom file folder where the month is, to change the name of the month. Make sure you always create a new month before you start changing data.

A budget generally consists of your current cash situation (Checking, Money Markets, Liquid Line of Credit, and Petty Cash) your asset situation on your Accounts Receivables, and your Liabilities including Accounts Payable, Loans Payable, Payroll, Payroll Taxes, and Credit Cards. If you can sit down and figure out a budget on a bi-weekly basis for your client, you would take their current cash, and add any Accounts Receivable, or if a cash basis, estimate their weekly cash sales. You would then take that figure and compare it to your current Accounts Payable Aging and Liabilities due in that time period. Estimate what bills can be paid when, how much cash you will need to cover payroll and taxes, and see your bottom line cash situation. If you're consistent with your budget, you can constantly be on top of it to avoid any unforeseen situations with Cash Flow Issues. Your client will definitely appreciate this, and they will be able to see in advance if the company is suffering from a cash flow situation, or if they are expecting a profit for the month.

Make sure you offer to create a personal budget for your clients as well. The personal expenditures seem to be the weakest point for small business owners. When this weakness of overspending happens, the business is the portion that takes the biggest hit with bigger draws, more credit card debt and uncontrollable spending. The best way to see what is going on, and why they are always living from month to month if this is a problem, is to start at the very beginning with their personal finances.

✓ Cleaning up Accounting and Bookkeeping

A very good moneymaker is cleaning up someone else's mess! There are so many incompetent accountants and bookkeepers claiming to produce quality work – however, you will soon find out that this is not true! You need to be able to walk into a potential client's office, review their business type, and complete an overview of what type of work needs to be implemented. This is definitely a confidence booster!

You will use the same principle in preparing an Audit as you would in cleaning up messy books. Start from scratch (normally the beginning of the year, unless they are being audited). You would take their prior year business tax return, and set up a new company and re-create a balance sheet in your QuickBooks Pro® database. After you enter in the data to form your balance sheet, you always start with organizing. It is too difficult to search through boxes and papers trying to find something over and over again. If the files are set up in the order they should be, cleaning up the mess is halfway over. Once the files are in order, you will start with the bank statements and canceled checks. You want to make sure your balance sheet accounts are all in balance. Call any banks and credit card companies to get copies of statements if you don't know the correct balance. Once you receive additional information, post the charges and interest as expenses and reconcile those accounts.

Always double-check someone else's payroll! If they don't have a payroll service, recommend one to them that sends you business! If they question why, just let them know that you can't beat the convenience and time of a payroll service and that you work well as together as a team!

✓ **Year End Accounting**

I have enclosed a Year End Checklist in the forms portion of this instruction manual to help guide you through processing year-end books. There are many things to take into consideration when finalizing a Year End. If you have a CPA preparing the tax returns for your clients (which I recommend, unless you plan on becoming an Enrolled Agent) then you can help save your client money by finalizing as much data as possible.

- Make sure all checking accounts are reconciled.
- Reconcile your Accounts Receivable and Accounts Payable. Make sure all invoicing and bills are posted (especially if they're on an accrual basis).
- Get all cash receipts from your client to post. If there were payments paid from the owner that related to business, they would be applied to their "Owner Contribution" account. That would reduce their personal cash payments and increase their expenses.
- If you have loans on your balance sheet, get the bank or lending institution to send you a year-end report with the balance to make sure they match. If they don't balance each other, it's generally due to interest expenses. You can create a journal entry posting the interest to your expense account, thus adjusting your loan amount to balance the bank records.
- Prepare and file 1099's. Hopefully throughout the year you have collected the W9 information on all of the contractors. If you have not, they need to be finalized and postmarked to the contractor no later than January 31st. The reports are due to the IRS by February 15th.
- Print out a YTD General Ledger. Go through each account and review everything in it. Make sure that each cash and loan account (checking, receivables, payables, notes, inventory, fixed assets) has backup documentation, to prove that their balances are correct. Review your income and expense accounts and verify that all of the expense checks, invoices and customer payments have been posted to the correct

account. If they have not, you need to make a journal entry re-posting the entries to the correct accounts.

- Reconcile your Payroll Reports! If you have a payroll service that handles the payroll, make sure your records balance each other. There is also another formula to check your figures.

- Take your State Unemployment Rate, and times it by your <u>gross</u> payroll, including salaries, hourly, and bonuses. If that number matches your expense account total for State Unemployment, your reports are correct.

- Do the same with Federal Unemployment, Social Security, and Medicare Tax. Each client's Unemployment rate could be different; it depends on how many times they terminate employees. The general rate for Social Security and Medicare is still 7.65% (1.45% Medicare and 6.20% for Social Security). When you multiply the percentage rates by the gross payroll and your book balance is the same, then your payroll is accurate.

- If it does not match, there was a posting error somewhere in the year. You will need to take the Gross Payroll Reported to the IRS and State from your payroll tax returns, and post a journal entry. Nine out of ten times, payroll fees were accidentally posted into your gross wage accounts, which caused the reports to be wrong. If you are over by a limited dollar amount and can't figure out where the amount came from, it is okay to make a journal entry adjusting your payroll expense accounts to balance with your tax reports, and apply the difference to miscellaneous expenses.

- Post your depreciation. Keep track of Fixed Assets, and the date they were acquired, and post them to your Fixed Asset account in full description. It will make your job much easier at the end of the year when you go to depreciate. Generally, the CPA firm will depreciate the assets anyway, but learn how to do it. Post the entry debiting (increasing) your expense account (called depreciation), and crediting (reducing) your balance sheet account (called accumulated depreciation). Generally you use the MACRS Straight Line Depreciation, for which I have included a copy of the formula. It is very simple to use. There are guidelines depending on what asset type it is, what its useful life expectancy is, and whether it was acquired in the middle or the end of the fiscal year. If you are preparing the tax return and use Turbo-Tax or software like it, it does calculate the value for you, but you should learn how to do it regardless.

- Most CPA Firms use QuickBooks Pro® as well. The majority of their clients are set up on QuickBooks Pro® (which is why I highly recommend that you do as well). This is a list of the following information that a CPA firm will require from you to prepare your client's tax returns.
    - Backup disk of client's books from QuickBooks Pro®
    - Hard copy of the following reports:
    - Balance Sheet (Current Year and Prior Year comparison if available)
    - YTD Financial Statement (Cash or Accrual depending on what the client files with the IRS and State)
    - YTD Payroll Tax Reports
    - You must also provide all of your client's _personal_ tax information (I guarantee they will give it to you to handle), such as:
    - Mortgage interest
    - Medical expenses
    - Donations
    - 1099's
- Generally the CPA will make the final year-end adjustment to the balance sheet to zero out the owner's distributions for the upcoming year. However, if you need to make this adjustment to the balance sheet, you need to post your entry to zero out the following accounts. If your client takes draws instead of a payroll check, that account needs to be zero as of January 1st of the new year. To close out the prior

year's books, you need to post a journal entry to Beginning Capital, Capital Draw or Distribution, Tax-Deductible (if not a corporation), and apply the balance of all the accounts zeroing out to your retained earnings account. This will be a clean fresh set of books for the new year.

✓ 1099 Miscellaneous Income

1099's are the IRS's way of keeping track of income for "General Contractors," "Consultants," and like you, a "Bookkeeper." The purpose for these tax forms is to keep independent contractors' income traced so they can't hide their earnings from the IRS. 1099's are only processed for **"Sole Proprietors,"** self-employed individuals earning a living in a **"service"** field. There is a maximum earning amount they have to receive from one company to qualify to receive a 1099. That amount is still **$600** per year. A Corporation or a LLC does not receive a 1099 miscellaneous income form.

When you are processing your client's records, whether it is manually entering in the checks they wrote for that month, or doing the accounts payable yourself, you always need to record and keep track of all independent contractors. Even if they receive a check for $300, which is below the limit, you still need to send them a W9-form (you can download the forms online from the IRS website, address located in the back of this book). If your client has an on-site accounts payable, you must supply the accounts payable with the W9, and inform them not to release payment to the contractor until that form is received with all of the proper information filled in. If you do the accounts payable yourself, you will need to make sure the contractor returns the W9 to you before you can issue a payment. If the contractor refuses to fill out the W9 form, you are required by Federal Regulations to withhold 31% from their payment and submit it to the IRS for Federal Taxes. The penalty for continuing to pay a contractor without filling their Tax ID number to the IRS is up to $100,000, and I really don't think your client would be happy about paying that.

If you keep track of the contractor's W9's throughout the year, you won't be rushing to obtain the information before the IRS due date for filing. The current due date for 1099's to the individual is the same as a W2, January 31st. The copy that goes to the IRS reporting agency is due by February 15th. It is always best to just send them both out by January 31st.

You can call the IRS directly to order any form or publication you may need, or order them online. It usually takes 7 to 15 days to receive your forms. Make sure you order enough in case of errors. The IRS does not supply computer-generated forms. If you want to be able to process them through QuickBooks Pro®, which I recommend, then go to your local office supply store or McBee Bookkeeping Systems and order computer-generated 1099's. It is much easier and less time consuming to print them from your accounting software then to type them in. **However**, when you purchase a package of 1099's from an office supply store, they only supply one (1) Form 1096, which is the annual tax summary that is the attachment form for the 1099's you are submitting. It is crucial that you order additional 1096 forms from the IRS; they do not accept a photocopy of this form as an original. (It's one of the few they don't accept, under the Paperwork Reduction Act.) Make sure you total your 1099's and they equal the amount you are submitting on your 1096 form. Keep a file folder containing all documentation (W9's) and the copy of the 1099 and 1096 Tax Return filed to the IRS for that fiscal year.

✓ Record Keeping

The following list is something that you need to make available for yourself and your clients as well. This is IRS and State regulation on the amount of time required to store documentation relating to your business.

Keep Forever:
- Tax Returns (IRS, State, Payroll, City, 1099)
- Bank Statements
- Canceled Checks
- Financial Statements that correspond to the tax returns.

- Bank Deposit Slips
- Daily Cash Receipt Folder (copies of the customer payments, plus the deposit slips)
- Payroll Reports and Payroll Taxes

The neatest invention is to be able to scan your records. This will free up your space and help save a tree. Once your items are even two years old, scan them in and keep a duplicate copy on a CD-ROM disk. You can then destroy your paper copies.

Keep for 7 Years:
- Accounts Receivable Invoices
- Accounts Payable Invoices (remember in the Audit Preparation section, I had to call vendors to locate invoices that were paid, to prove where the money went? It is important to hold onto these items until you are out of audit range. Otherwise your client will not be able to use that deduction, if they can't prove where it went even if they have a canceled check).
- Bank Notes (unless they are longer than a 5- or 7-year note) Use your best judgment on this one.

QuickBooks Pro® **Sample Company "Rock Castle Construction"**

The following reports were created from the QuickBooks Pro® sample company. I recreated the company from the QuickBooks Pro® original "sample company" to show you how to make a journal entry when you take over another bookkeeping service's client. The chart of accounts is in the format that I use, along with the attached forms that you should get familiar with. Computers do wonders for record-keeping and for reducing the amount of time it takes to keep track of accounting data; however, you still need hard copies in case your computer crashes and your backup disks won't reload. Trust me, it can happen! The attached reports are based on my recreation of Rock Castle Construction Company.

Balance Sheet

Profit and Loss Statement

General Ledger

Trial Balance

Journal Entry

Chart of Accounts

When restoring the Rock Castle Construction backup disks, keep in mind it is from the QuickBooks Pro® 2002 version. I purposely did not update this disk to the most current version of QuickBooks® because in doing so, only the customers who had the most current version would be able to open it. You can always update the data file from an older version to a newer version, but you cannot regress the versions to communicate.

Rock Castle Construction
Balance Sheet
As of September 30, 2008

	Sep 30, 08
ASSETS	
Current Assets	
Checking/Savings	
Checking	9,276.28
Savings	29,500.00
Total Checking/Savings	38,776.28
Accounts Receivable	
Accounts Receivable	31,898.13
Total Accounts Receivable	31,898.13
Other Current Assets	
Tools & Equipment	5,000.00
Inventory Asset	4,391.88
Undeposited Funds	34,197.88
Total Other Current Assets	43,589.76
Total Current Assets	114,264.17
Fixed Assets	
Trucks	
Original Cost	33,852.91
Depreciation	-9,000.00
Total Trucks	24,852.91
Total Fixed Assets	24,852.91
Other Assets	
Pre-paid Insurance	2,025.00
Total Other Assets	2,025.00
TOTAL ASSETS	**141,142.08**
LIABILITIES & EQUITY	
Liabilities	
Current Liabilities	
Accounts Payable	
Accounts Payable	3,158.28
Total Accounts Payable	3,158.28
Credit Cards	
CalOil Card	65.88
Total Credit Cards	65.88
Other Current Liabilities	
Payroll Liabilities	3,781.99
Sales Tax Payable	4,536.41
Total Other Current Liabilities	8,318.40

We will use this balance sheet supplied to us by our client to re-create our clients set of books in QuickBooks Pro ®. Make sure you verify all information and account balances to assure accuracy. If you need additional documentation, ask!

Undeposited funds are money received for services that have been applied against your open customer invoices but have not yet been deposited to your bank account.

Depreciation is booked in monthly as well. See the chapter on Depreciation.

Prepaid expenses need to be accounted for like depreciation in a sense. You can't write it off until you use it. One year premium would be a monthly journal entry of $168.75 per month for Insurance Expense. You would reduce this account each month for 12 months until it is zero to account for the expense.

Payroll Tax Liabilites should be broken down by item. FICA, Medicare, Fed Witholding, etc. One balance doesn't give you enough information.

Rock Castle Construction
Balance Sheet
As of September 30, 2008

	Sep 30, 08
Total Current Liabilities	11,542.56
Long Term Liabilities	
Note Payable	20,500.00
Truck Loan	7,149.32
Total Long Term Liabilities	27,649.32
Total Liabilities	39,191.88
Equity	
Opening Bal Equity	8,863.39
Owner's Equity	
Owner's Contribution	25,000.00
Total Owner's Equity	25,000.00
Retained Earnings	-8,639.96
Net Income	76,726.77
Total Equity	101,950.20
TOTAL LIABILITIES & EQUITY	141,142.08

Make sure your Total Assets and Total Liabilties balance out.

Rock Castle Construction
Profit & Loss
October 2007 through September 2008

	Oct '07 - Sep 08
Ordinary Income/Expense	
Income	
Construction	
Discounts given	-48.35
Labor	43,950.50
Materials	49,959.34
Miscellaneous	4,245.10
Subcontractors	37,170.30
Total Construction	135,276.89
Total Income	135,276.89
Cost of Goods Sold	
Cost of Goods Sold	2,515.26
Total COGS	2,515.26
Gross Profit	132,761.63
Expense	
Automobile	
Insurance	2,850.24
Repairs and Maintenance	942.90
Total Automobile	3,793.14
Depreciation Expense	3,000.00
Freight & Delivery	0.00
Insurance	
Disability Insurance	450.00
Liability Insurance	3,150.00
Work Comp	2,475.00
Total Insurance	6,075.00
Interest Expense	708.12
Job Expenses	
Equipment Rental	850.00
Job Materials	26,527.62
Subcontractors	11,146.95
Total Job Expenses	38,524.57
Tools and Machinery	2,470.68
Utilities	
Gas and Electric	887.08
Telephone	576.27
Total Utilities	1,463.35
Total Expense	56,034.86
Net Ordinary Income	76,726.77
Net Income	**76,726.77**

> Your clients fiscal year is from October 1st through September 30th. If your reports aren't run between that date range, your balance sheet net income won't match your income statement. Make sure when you set up Quickbooks you are in the correct fiscal year.

> Net Income Matches Balance Sheets Net income.

Accrual Basis

Rock Castle Construction
Trial Balance
As of September 30, 2008

	Sep 30, 08	
	Debit	Credit
Checking	9,276.28	
Savings	29,500.00	
Accounts Receivable	31,898.13	
Tools & Equipment	5,000.00	
Inventory Asset	4,391.88	
Undeposited Funds	34,197.88	
Trucks:Original Cost	33,852.91	
Trucks:Depreciation		9,000.00
Pre-paid Insurance	2,025.00	
Accounts Payable		3,158.28
CalOil Card		65.88
Payroll Liabilities		3,781.99
Sales Tax Payable		4,536.41
Note Payable		20,500.00
Truck Loan		7,149.32
Opening Bal Equity		8,863.39
Owner's Equity:Owner's Contribution		25,000.00
Retained Earnings	8,639.96	
Construction:Discounts given	48.35	
Construction:Labor		43,950.50
Construction:Materials		49,959.34
Construction:Miscellaneous		4,245.10
Construction:Subcontractors		37,170.30
Cost of Goods Sold	2,515.26	
Automobile:Insurance	2,850.24	
Automobile:Repairs and Maintenance	942.90	
Depreciation Expense	3,000.00	
Freight & Delivery	0.00	
Insurance:Disability Insurance	450.00	
Insurance:Liability Insurance	3,150.00	
Insurance:Work Comp	2,475.00	
Interest Expense	708.12	
Job Expenses:Equipment Rental	850.00	
Job Expenses:Job Materials	26,527.62	
Job Expenses:Subcontractors	11,146.95	
Tools and Machinery	2,470.68	
Utilities:Gas and Electric	887.08	
Utilities:Telephone	576.27	
TOTAL	**217,380.51**	**217,380.51**

These chart of accounts don't describe the detail of work, so we will change them on our set-up of the construction company. At this point a journal entry to room additions is the majority of our contractors work, so we will post it the total of $135,325.24 of construction income to account 1350.01

Accounts Payable Journal Entry Summary

	Total Exp	A/P aging	Net Exp
Accounts payable			
Automobile:Insurance	2,850.24	0	2,850.24
Automobile:Repairs and Maintenanc	942.90	0	942.90
Depreciation Expense	3,000.00	0	3,000.00
Freight & Delivery	0.00	0	0.00
Insurance:Disability Insurance	450.00	0	450.00
Insurance:Liability Insurance	3,150.00	0	3,150.00
Insurance:Work Comp	2,475.00	0	2,475.00
Interest Expense	708.12	0	708.12
Job Expenses:Equipment Rental	850.00	0	850.00
Job Expenses:Job Materials	26,527.62	-1093.5	**25,434.12**
Job Expenses:Subcontractors	11,146.95	-1947	**9,199.95**
Tools and Machinery	2,470.68	0	2,470.68
Utilities:Gas and Electric	887.08	0	887.08
Utilities:Telephone	576.27	-117.78	**458.49**
	56034.86	-3158.28	

This is your new journal entry amount for Job Materials Account 1375.02

This is your new journal entry amount for subcontracted labor account 1375.04

This is your new journal entry amount for telephone Account 1480

which equals that total outstanding on your accounts payable. Don't forget to re-enter the bills into quickbooks by selecting vendor, enter bills. That way your accounts payable is correct.

Rock Castle Construction
A/P Aging Summary
As of September 30, 2008

	Current	1 - 30	31 - 60	61 - 90	> 90	TOTAL
Cal Telephone	68.35	49.43	0.00	0.00	0.00	117.78
McClain Appliances	455.50	0.00	0.00	0.00	0.00	455.50
Sloan Roofing	500.00	0.00	0.00	0.00	850.00	1,350.00
Timberloft Lumber	638.00	0.00	0.00	0.00	0.00	638.00
Washuta & Son Painting	597.00	0.00	0.00	0.00	0.00	597.00
TOTAL	2,258.85	49.43	0.00	0.00	850.00	3,158.28

Opening journal entry to reduce accounts payable under the Cost of Goods Materials account 1375.02

Opening journal entry to reduce accounts payable under telephone expense account 1480

Opening journal entry to reduce accounts payable under the Sub-Contracted Labor Account 1375.04

Opening journal entry to reduce accounts payable under the Sub-Contracted Labor Account 1375.04

Opening journal entry to reduce accounts payable under the Cost of Goods Materials account 1375.02

The Opening Journal Entry will be changed from the $3,158.28 originally applied to the accounts payable according to the trial balance and will reduce your expense accounts because your expenses are booked in already on the trial balance. Once you input the vendor bills that are still due, your accounts payable will total the $3,158.28 and your expense accounts will once again equal the total on your trial balance. The reason why we aren't including the accounts payable on your opening Journal entry is because your client is on an accrual basis and you will need to pay those bills. So we want to keep accurate track of their payables by re-entering them into his system.

Accounts Receivable Journal Entry Summary

Trial Balance Entry from old Bookkeeper

Construction:Labor	48.35
Construction:Materials	43,950.50
Construction:Miscellaneous	49,959.34
Construction:Subcontractors	4,245.10
	37,170.30
	135,276.89 Total Income per old Trial Balance

Our Journal Entry	**Income**	**Total A/R**	**Net Entry**
construction: Room Additions	135,276.89	-31,898.13	**103,378.76**

This is your new journal entry total. The difference between the total income less what is due on the accounts receivable books. Once you re-enter your invoices into Quickbooks, your total revenue will once again be $135,325.24. Enter it to account 1350.01

Accounts Receivable Summary

	Current	1 - 30	31 - 60	61 - 90	> 90	TOTAL
Burch, Jason						
Room Addition	5,912.93	0.00	0.00	0.00	0.00	5,912.93
Total Burch, Jason	5,912.93	0.00	0.00	0.00	0.00	5,912.93
Memeo, Jeanette						
2nd story addition	14,538.54	0.00	0.00	0.00	0.00	14,538.54
Utility Shed	0.00	0.00	1,999.00	0.00	0.00	1,999.00
Total Memeo, Jeanette	14,538.54	0.00	1,999.00	0.00	0.00	16,537.54
Nguyen, Tuan						
Garage	0.00	4,819.00	0.00	0.00	0.00	4,819.00
Total Nguyen, Tuan	0.00	4,819.00	0.00	0.00	0.00	4,819.00
Smith, Lee						
Patio	5.00	4,623.66	0.00	0.00	0.00	4,628.66
Total Smith, Lee	5.00	4,623.66	0.00	0.00	0.00	4,628.66
TOTAL	20,456.47	9,442.66	1,999.00	0.00	0.00	31,898.13

Opening Accounts Receivable journal entry is going to reduce the Exterior Structures Income account 1350.03

Opening Accounts Receivable journal entry is going to reduce the Room Additions Income account 1350.01

Opening Accounts Receivable journal entry is going to reduce the Exterior Structures Income account 1350.03

The Opening Journal Entry will be changed from the $31,898.13 originally applied to the accounts receivable according to the trial balance and will reduce your income accounts because your income is already booked in on the trial balance. Once you input the customers invoices that are still due, your accounts receivable will total the $31,898.13 and your income accounts will once again equal the total on your trial balance. The reason why we aren't including the accounts receivable on your opening Journal entry is because your client is on an accrual basis and you will need receive and track the accounts receivable still due to your client. That way you can run an aging showing all of the invoices that are outstanding and they don't forget who owes them money.

Rock Castle Construction
Opening Journal Entry
October 2007 through September 2008

Trans #	Type	Date	Num	Name	Memo	Account	Debit	Credit
2	General Jou	09/30/2003	0903-001		R/C Opening Balance	1100 · Checking	9,276.28	
					R/C Opening Balance	1101 · Savings	29,500.00	
					R/C Opening Balance	1130 · Undeposited funds	34,197.88	
					R/C Opening Balance	1150.02 · Vehicles	33,852.91	
					R/C Opening Balance	1150.04 · Accum Deprec		9,000.00
					R/C Opening Balance	1200.02 · CalOil Card		65.88
					R/C Opening Balance	1250 · Payroll Liabilities		3,781.99
					R/C Opening Balance	1280 · Sales Tax Payable		4,536.41
					R/C Opening Balance	1285.01 · Truck Loan		20,500.00
					R/C Opening Balance	1285.02 · Other Notes		7,149.32
					R/C Opening Balance	1300 · Opening Bal Equity		8,863.39
					R/C Opening Balance	1305 · Retained Earnings	8,639.96	
					R/C Opening Balance	1120 · Inventory Asset	4,391.88	
					R/C Opening Balance	1150.03 · Tools & Equipment	5,000.00	
					R/C Opening Balance	1125.02 · Insurance	2,025.00	
					R/C Opening Balance	1304.01 · Owners Contribution		25,000.00
					R/C Opening Balance	1350.05 · Discounts Given	48.35	
					R/C Opening Balance	1350.01 · Room Additions		103,427.11
					R/C Opening Balance	1375 · Cost of Goods Sold	2,515.26	
					R/C Opening Balance	1402.03 · Inusrance	2,850.24	
					R/C Opening Balance	1402.01 · Repairs & Maint	942.90	
					R/C Opening Balance	1407 · Depreciation Expense	3,000.00	
					R/C Opening Balance	1417.01 · Disability Insurance	450.00	
					R/C Opening Balance	1417.02 · Liability Insurance	3,150.00	
					R/C Opening Balance	1417.03 · Workers Comp	2,475.00	
					R/C Opening Balance	1411 · Interest Expense	708.12	
					R/C Opening Balance	1375.06 · Equipment Rental	850.00	
					R/C Opening Balance	1375.02 · Job Materials	25,434.12	
					R/C Opening Balance	1375.04 · Subcontractors	9,199.95	
					R/C Opening Balance	1375.05 · Tools & Machinery	2,470.68	
					R/C Opening Balance	1495.01 · Gas and Electric	887.08	
					R/C Opening Balance	1480 · Telephone	458.49	
							182,324.10	182,324.10
6	Bill	09/01/2003		Cal Telephone		1175 · Accounts Payables		117.78
				Cal Telephone	Telephone	1480 · Telephone	117.78	
							117.78	117.78
7	Bill	09/01/2003		McClain Appliances		1175 · Accounts Payables		455.50
				McClain Appliances	Job Materials	1375.02 · Job Materials	455.50	
							455.50	455.50
8	Bill	06/01/2003		Sloan Roofing		1175 · Accounts Payables		850.00
				Sloan Roofing		1375.04 · Subcontractors	850.00	
							850.00	850.00
9	Bill	09/01/2003		Sloan Roofing		1175 · Accounts Payables		500.00
				Sloan Roofing		1350.03 · Exterior Structures	500.00	
							500.00	500.00
10	Bill	09/01/2003		Timberloft Lumber		1175 · Accounts Payables		638.00
				Timberloft Lumber		1375.02 · Job Materials	638.00	
							638.00	638.00
11	Bill	09/01/2003		Washuta & Son Painting		1175 · Accounts Payables		597.00
				Washuta & Son Painting		1350.03 · Exterior Structures	597.00	
							597.00	597.00
12	Invoice	09/01/2003	1	Burch, Jason		1110 · Accounts Receivable	5,912.93	
				Burch, Jason	Room Additions	1350.01 · Room Additions		5,912.93
							5,912.93	5,912.93

This is your adjusting journal entry to set up your clients new set of books from another bookkeeping service.

13	Invoice	09/01/2003	2	Memeo, Jeanette		1110 · Accounts Receivable	14,538.54	
				Memeo, Jeanette	2nd story Room Additions	1350.01 · Room Additions		14,538.54
							14,538.54	14,538.54
14	Invoice	09/01/2003	3	Nguyen, Tuan		1110 · Accounts Receivable	4,819.00	
				Nguyen, Tuan	Exterior Construction	1350.03 · Exterior Structures		4,819.00
							4,819.00	4,819.00
15	Invoice	09/01/2003	4	Smith, Lee		1110 · Accounts Receivable	4,623.66	
				Smith, Lee	Patio Exterior Construction	1350.03 · Exterior Structures		4,623.66
							4,623.66	4,623.66
16	Invoice	09/01/2003	5	Smith, Lee		1110 · Accounts Receivable	5.00	
				Smith, Lee	Exterior Construction	1350.03 · Exterior Structures		5.00
							5.00	5.00
17	Invoice	07/01/2003	6	Memeo, Jeanette		1110 · Accounts Receivable	1,999.00	
				Memeo, Jeanette	Utility Shed Exterior Constructic	1350.03 · Exterior Structures		1,999.00
							1,999.00	1,999.00
							217,380.51	**217,380.51**

Rock Castle Construction
Balance Sheet
As of September 30, 2008

BALANCE SHEET - RE-CREATED TO NEW BOOKS

	Sep 30, 08
ASSETS	
Current Assets	
Checking/Savings	
1100 · Checking	9,276.28
1101 · Savings	29,500.00
Total Checking/Savings	38,776.28
Accounts Receivable	
1110 · Accounts Receivable	31,898.13
Total Accounts Receivable	31,898.13
Other Current Assets	
1120 · Inventory Asset	4,391.88
1125 · Prepaid Expenses	
1125.02 · Insurance	2,025.00
Total 1125 · Prepaid Expenses	2,025.00
1130 · Undeposited funds	34,197.88
Total Other Current Assets	40,614.76
Total Current Assets	111,289.17
Fixed Assets	
1150 · Fixed Asset	
1150.02 · Vehicles	33,852.91
1150.03 · Tools & Equipment	5,000.00
1150.04 · Accumulated Depreciation	-9,000.00
Total 1150 · Fixed Asset	29,852.91
Total Fixed Assets	29,852.91
TOTAL ASSETS	141,142.08
LIABILITIES & EQUITY	
Liabilities	
Current Liabilities	
Accounts Payable	
1175 · Accounts Payables	3,158.28
Total Accounts Payable	3,158.28
Credit Cards	
1200 · Credit Card	
1200.02 · CalOil Card	65.88
Total 1200 · Credit Card	65.88
Total Credit Cards	65.88

> This is what our new balance sheet is going to look like. Make sure the beginning balances match.

> Total Assets & Liabilities match prior bookkeepers balance sheet. Everything is correct

109

Rock Castle Construction
Balance Sheet
As of September 30, 2008

	Sep 30, 08
Other Current Liabilities	
1250 · Payroll Liabilities	3,781.99
1280 · Sales Tax Payable	4,536.41
1285 · Notes Payable	
1285.01 · Truck Loan	7,149.32
1285.02 · Other Notes	20,500.00
Total 1285 · Notes Payable	27,649.32
Total Other Current Liabilities	35,967.72
Total Current Liabilities	39,191.88
Total Liabilities	39,191.88
Equity	
1300 · Opening Bal Equity	8,863.39
1304 · Owner's Capital	
1304.01 · Owners Contribution	25,000.00
Total 1304 · Owner's Capital	25,000.00
1305 · Retained Earnings	-8,639.96
Net Income	76,726.77
Total Equity	101,950.20
TOTAL LIABILITIES & EQUITY	141,142.08

110

PROFIT AND LOSS - RE-CREATED TO NEW BOOKS

	Oct '07 - Sep 08
Ordinary Income/Expense	
Income	
1350 · Construction	
1350.01 · Room Additions	123,878.58
1350.03 · Exterior Structures	11,446.66
1350.05 · Discounts Given	-48.35
Total 1350 · Construction	135,276.89
Total Income	135,276.89
Cost of Goods Sold	
1375 · Cost of Goods Sold	
1375.02 · Job Materials	26,527.62
1375.04 · Subcontractors	11,146.95
1375.05 · Tools and Machinery	2,470.68
1375.06 · Equipment Rental	850.00
1375 · Cost of Goods Sold - Other	2,515.26
Total 1375 · Cost of Goods Sold	43,510.51
Total COGS	43,510.51
Gross Profit	91,766.38
Expense	
1402 · Automobile Expense	
1402.03 · Inusrance	2,850.24
1402.01 · Repairs & Maintenance	942.90
Total 1402 · Automobile Expense	3,793.14
1407 · Depreciation Expense	3,000.00
1411 · Interest Expense	708.12
1417 · Insurance	
1417.01 · Disability Insurance	450.00
1417.02 · Liability Insurance	3,150.00
1417.03 · Workers Compensation	2,475.00
Total 1417 · Insurance	6,075.00
1480 · Telephone	576.27
1495 · Utilities	
1495.01 · Gas and Electric	887.08
Total 1495 · Utilities	887.08
Total Expense	15,039.61
Net Ordinary Income	76,726.77
Net Income	76,726.77

> Our gross profit is different from the old bookkeepers because Job expenses are a Cost of Goods and should be accounted accordingly. We moved the Job expenses from our expense accounts to our COG chart of accounts thus reflecting a difference in Gross Profit.

> Net Income Matches Balance Sheets Net income on both new and old set of books.

Rock Castle Construction
Trial Balance
As of September 30, 2008

TRIAL BALANCE - RECREATED TO NEW BOOKS

	Sep 30, 08	
	Debit	Credit
1100 · Checking	9,276.28	
1101 · Savings	29,500.00	
1110 · Accounts Receivable	31,898.13	
1120 · Inventory Asset	4,391.88	
1125 · Prepaid Expenses:1125.02 · Insurance	2,025.00	
1130 · Undeposited funds	34,197.88	
1150 · Fixed Asset:1150.02 · Vehicles	33,852.91	
1150 · Fixed Asset:1150.03 · Tools & Equipment	5,000.00	
1150 · Fixed Asset:1150.04 · Accumulated Depreciation		9,000.00
1175 · Accounts Payables		3,158.28
1200 · Credit Card:1200.02 · CalOil Card		65.88
1250 · Payroll Liabilities		3,781.99
1280 · Sales Tax Payable		4,536.41
1285 · Notes Payable:1285.01 · Truck Loan		20,500.00
1285 · Notes Payable:1285.02 · Other Notes		7,149.32
1300 · Opening Bal Equity		8,863.39
1304 · Owner's Capital:1304.01 · Owners Contribution		25,000.00
1305 · Retained Earnings	8,639.96	
1350 · Construction:1350.01 · Room Additions		123,878.58
1350 · Construction:1350.03 · Exterior Structures		11,446.66
1350 · Construction:1350.05 · Discounts Given	48.35	
1375 · Cost of Goods Sold	2,515.26	
1375 · Cost of Goods Sold:1375.02 · Job Materials	26,527.62	
1375 · Cost of Goods Sold:1375.04 · Subcontractors	11,146.95	
1375 · Cost of Goods Sold:1375.05 · Tools and Machinery	2,470.68	
1375 · Cost of Goods Sold:1375.06 · Equipment Rental	850.00	
1402 · Automobile Expense:1402.03 · Inusrance	2,850.24	
1402 · Automobile Expense:1402.01 · Repairs & Maintenance	942.90	
1407 · Depreciation Expense	3,000.00	
1411 · Interest Expense	708.12	
1417 · Insurance:1417.01 · Disability Insurance	450.00	
1417 · Insurance:1417.02 · Liability Insurance	3,150.00	
1417 · Insurance:1417.03 · Workers Compensation	2,475.00	
1480 · Telephone	576.27	
1495 · Utilities:1495.01 · Gas and Electric	887.08	
TOTAL	217,380.51	217,380.51

Our A/R and A/P are re-entered in and show the accurate aging balance due.

Our COG accounts are broken down into sub-accounts for a more descriptive analysis.

GENERAL LEDGER	Date	Num	Name	Memo	Debit	Credit	Balance
1100 · Checking							0.00
	09/30/2003	0903-001		R/C Opening Balance	9,276.28		9,276.28
Total 1100 · Checking					9,276.28	0.00	9,276.28
1101 · Savings							0.00
	09/30/2003	0903-001		R/C Opening Balance	29,500.00		29,500.00
Total 1101 · Savings					29,500.00	0.00	29,500.00
1110 · Accounts Receivable							0.00
	07/01/2003	6	Memeo, Jeanette	We re-entered in each invoice to account for what is due on your accounts receivable aging.	1,999.00		1,999.00
	09/01/2003	1	Burch, Jason		5,912.93		7,911.93
	09/01/2003	2	Memeo, Jeanette		14,538.54		22,450.47
	09/01/2003	3	Nguyen, Tuan		4,819.00		27,269.47
	09/01/2003	4	Smith, Lee		4,623.66		31,893.13
	09/01/2003	5	Smith, Lee		5.00		31,898.13
Total 1110 · Accounts Receivable					31,898.13	0.00	31,898.13
1120 · Inventory Asset							0.00
	09/30/2003	0903-001		R/C Opening Balance	4,391.88		4,391.88
Total 1120 · Inventory Asset					4,391.88	0.00	4,391.88
1125 · Prepaid Expenses							0.00
1125.02 · Insurance							0.00
	09/30/2003	0903-001		R/C Opening Balance	2,025.00		2,025.00
Total 1125.02 · Insurance					2,025.00	0.00	2,025.00
Total 1125 · Prepaid Expenses					2,025.00	0.00	2,025.00
1130 · Undeposited funds							0.00
	09/30/2003	0903-001		R/C Opening Balance	34,197.88		34,197.88
Total 1130 · Undeposited funds					34,197.88	0.00	34,197.88
1150 · Fixed Asset							0.00
1150.02 · Vehicles							0.00
	09/30/2003	0903-001		R/C Opening Balance	33,852.91		33,852.91
Total 1150.02 · Vehicles					33,852.91	0.00	33,852.91
1150.03 · Tools & Equipment							0.00
	09/30/2003	0903-001		R/C Opening Balance	5,000.00		5,000.00
Total 1150.03 · Tools & Equipment					5,000.00	0.00	5,000.00
1150.04 · Accumulated Depreciation							0.00
	09/30/2003	0903-001		R/C Opening Balance		9,000.00	-9,000.00
Total 1150.04 · Accumulated Depreciation					0.00	9,000.00	-9,000.00
Total 1150 · Fixed Asset					38,852.91	9,000.00	29,852.91
1175 · Accounts Payables							0.00
	06/01/2003		Sloan Roofing	We re-entered in each bill to account for what payables are still due.		850.00	-850.00
	09/01/2003		Cal Telephone			117.78	-967.78
	09/01/2003		McClain Appliances			455.50	-1,423.28
	09/01/2003		Sloan Roofing			500.00	-1,923.28
	09/01/2003		Timberloft Lumber			638.00	-2,561.28
	09/01/2003		Washuta & Son Painting			597.00	-3,158.28
Total 1175 · Accounts Payables					0.00	3,158.28	-3,158.28
1200 · Credit Card							0.00
1200.02 · CalOil Card							0.00
	09/30/2003	0903-001		R/C Opening Balance		65.88	-65.88
Total 1200.02 · CalOil Card					0.00	65.88	-65.88
Total 1200 · Credit Card					0.00	65.88	-65.88
1250 · Payroll Liabilities							0.00
	09/30/2003	0903-001		R/C Opening Balance		3,781.99	-3,781.99
Total 1250 · Payroll Liabilities					0.00	3,781.99	-3,781.99
1280 · Sales Tax Payable							0.00
	09/30/2003	0903-001		R/C Opening Balance		4,536.41	-4,536.41
Total 1280 · Sales Tax Payable					0.00	4,536.41	-4,536.41

GENERAL LEDGER	Date	Num	Name	Memo	Debit	Credit	Balance
1285 · Notes Payable							0.00
1285.01 · Truck Loan							0.00
	09/30/2003	0903-001		R/C Opening Balance		7,149.32	-20,500.00
Total 1285.01 · Truck Loan					0.00	7,149.32	-20,500.00
1285.02 · Other Notes							0.00
	09/30/2003	0903-001		R/C Opening Balance		20,500.00	-7,149.32
Total 1285.02 · Other Notes					0.00	20,500.00	-7,149.32
Total 1285 · Notes Payable					0.00	27,649.32	-27,649.32
1300 · Opening Bal Equity							0.00
	09/30/2003	0903-001		R/C Opening Balance		8,863.39	-8,863.39
Total 1300 · Opening Bal Equity					0.00	8,863.39	-8,863.39
1304 · Owner's Capital							0.00
1304.01 · Owners Contribution							0.00
	09/30/2003	0903-001		R/C Opening Balance		25,000.00	-25,000.00
Total 1304.01 · Owners Contribution					0.00	25,000.00	-25,000.00
Total 1304 · Owner's Capital					0.00	25,000.00	-25,000.00
1305 · Retained Earnings							0.00
Total 1305 · Retained Earnings					8,639.96	0.00	8,639.96
1350 · Construction							0.00
1350.01 · Room Additions							0.00
	09/01/2003	1	Burch, Jason	Room Additions		5,912.93	-5,912.93
	09/01/2003	2	Memeo, Jeanette	2nd story Room Additions		14,538.54	-20,451.47
	09/30/2003	0903-001		R/C Opening Balance		103,427.11	-123,878.58
Total 1350.01 · Room Additions					0.00	123,878.58	-123,878.58
1350.03 · Exterior Structures							0.00
	07/01/2003	6	Memeo, Jeanette	Utility Shed Exterior Construction		1,999.00	-1,999.00
	09/01/2003	3	Nguyen, Tuan	Exterior Construction		4,819.00	-6,818.00
	09/01/2003	4	Smith, Lee	Patio Exterior Construction		4,623.66	-11,441.66
	09/01/2003	5	Smith, Lee	Exterior Construction		5.00	-11,446.66
Total 1350.03 · Exterior Structures					0.00	11,446.66	-11,446.66
1350.05 · Discounts Given							0.00
	09/30/2003	0903-001		R/C Opening Balance	48.35		48.35
Total 1350.05 · Discounts Given					48.35	0.00	48.35
Total 1350 · Construction					48.35	135,325.24	-135,276.89
1375 · Cost of Goods Sold							0.00
1375.02 · Job Materials							0.00
	09/01/2003		McClain Appliances	Job Materials	455.50		455.50
	09/01/2003		Timberloft Lumber		638.00		1,093.50
	09/30/2003	0903-001		R/C Opening Balance	25,434.12		26,527.62
Total 1375.02 · Job Materials					26,527.62	0.00	26,527.62
1375.04 · Subcontractors							0.00
	06/01/2003		Sloan Roofing		850.00		850.00
	09/01/2003		Sloan Roofing		500.00		500.00
	09/01/2003		Washuta & Son Painting		597.00		597.00
	09/30/2003	0903-001		R/C Opening Balance	9,199.95		9,199.95
Total 1375.04 · Subcontractors					11,146.95	0.00	11,146.95
1375.05 · Tools and Machinery							0.00
	09/30/2003	0903-001		R/C Opening Balance	2,470.68		2,470.68
Total 1375.05 · Tools and Machinery					2,470.68	0.00	2,470.68
1375.06 · Equipment Rental							0.00
	09/30/2003	0903-001		R/C Opening Balance	850.00		850.00
Total 1375.06 · Equipment Rental					850.00	0.00	850.00
1375 · Cost of Goods Sold - Other							0.00
	09/30/2003	0903-001		R/C Opening Balance	2,515.26		2,515.26
Total 1375 · Cost of Goods Sold - Other					2,515.26	0.00	2,515.26

Always request a copy of the note so you can calculate the interest and have an accurate opening balance

Here is where your double entry bookkeeping is accounting for your accounts receivable invoices

Our Accounts payable double entry bookkeeping is debiting our cost of goods and crediting our accounts payable account.

GENERAL LEDGER	Date	Num	Name	Memo	Debit	Credit	Balance
Total 1375 · Cost of Goods Sold					43,510.51	0.00	43,510.51
1402 · Automobile Expense							0.00
1402.03 · Inusrance							0.00
	09/30/2003	0903-001		R/C Opening Balance	2,850.24		2,850.24
Total 1402.03 · Inusrance					2,850.24	0.00	2,850.24
1402.01 · Repairs & Maintenance							0.00
	09/30/2003	0903-001		R/C Opening Balance	942.90		942.90
Total 1402.01 · Repairs & Maintenance					942.90	0.00	942.90
Total 1402 · Automobile Expense					3,793.14	0.00	3,793.14
1407 · Depreciation Expense							0.00
	09/30/2003	0903-001		R/C Opening Balance	3,000.00		3,000.00
Total 1407 · Depreciation Expense					3,000.00	0.00	3,000.00
1411 · Interest Expense							0.00
	09/30/2003	0903-001		R/C Opening Balance	708.12		708.12
Total 1411 · Interest Expense					708.12	0.00	708.12
1417 · Insurance							0.00
1417.01 · Disability Insurance							0.00
	09/30/2003	0903-001		R/C Opening Balance	450.00		450.00
Total 1417.01 · Disability Insurance					450.00	0.00	450.00
1417.02 · Liability Insurance							0.00
	09/30/2003	0903-001		R/C Opening Balance	3,150.00		3,150.00
Total 1417.02 · Liability Insurance					3,150.00	0.00	3,150.00
1417.03 · Workers Compensation							0.00
	09/30/2003	0903-001		R/C Opening Balance	2,475.00		2,475.00
Total 1417.03 · Workers Compensation					2,475.00	0.00	2,475.00
Total 1417 · Insurance					6,075.00	0.00	6,075.00
1480 · Telephone							0.00
	09/01/2003		Cal Telephone	Telephone	117.78		117.78
	09/30/2003	0903-001		R/C Opening Balance	458.49		576.27
Total 1480 · Telephone					576.27	0.00	576.27
1495 · Utilities							0.00
1495.01 · Gas and Electric							0.00
	09/30/2003	0903-001		R/C Opening Balance	887.08		887.08
Total 1495.01 · Gas and Electric					887.08	0.00	887.08
Total 1495 · Utilities					887.08	0.00	887.08
TOTAL					217,380.51	217,380.51	0.00

Chapter 5
Preparing Taxes and Depreciation

✓ Preparing your own Taxes

Before you begin preparing tax returns, if you don't already know how, I **highly** suggest that you take a tax course. The best available tax courses that I have taken are offered by H&R Block. Their tax classes usually begin in September of every year. Their course isn't cheap though. It costs approximately $345, and the course lasts about eight weeks. It is a very in-depth class that provides you with excellent study materials and resources to learn how to prepare individual and small business tax returns. They cover depreciation, itemized deductions, all the way to IRA's. I truly believe that this course is worth the money. There are also other resources that you can use to take classes for tax preparation, such as:

> ➢ Community College programs (usually $30 per class)
> ➢ Jackson Hewitt Tax Preparers also offer a class

You need to think of yourself as a client, as well, by taking care of your books and preparing for the end of the year. Tax returns are like taking a test. Nobody likes to fail, and failure always means that you prepared them incorrectly. If you are not going to prepare tax returns including your own, even though your selected networking CPA will be more expensive than H&R Block, send it their way because you'll make up the difference in referrals. If you decide to do your own tax returns, make sure you use the year-end checklist included with this book as you would for any other clients. You don't want to forget any deductions especially if you know you are going to owe money. The first year of business is always a guessing game. Guess how much you're going to make. You don't know, and the IRS and most States give you an allowance the first year for underpayment of estimated taxes – which means they don't penalize you for not paying in enough. If you don't take my advice by analyzing each quarter of your business as you would for a client, by seeing how much money you actually made, then there is your first mistake. You can go into TurboTax® or whatever software you choose and plug in your numbers throughout the year to see what your tax liability is. It's always a dummy tax return, but it will keep you up to date on what you owe. You can then print out Estimated Tax payment coupons and if you have the money, send them in when they are due to avoid any problems at all. Or you can hurry up and file your tax return by January 31st and send the entire amount due without having any penalties at all. My suggestion is to keep on top of it throughout the year so you don't have any surprises, because you would then be killing yourself, the messenger. Self Employment Tax is the biggest portion of your Federal tax liability and it is also the one that always gets you. Your Self Employment Tax is only calculated on your Net Profits, so after all of your deductions (including Depreciation and your Home Office Deduction) are accounted for, that is your bottom-line Net Profit. All it really is, is your FICA and Medicare along with the Company match which equals 15.3%. They have to get their money somehow.

A Sole Proprietorship (Schedule C) is easy to do. You don't have to worry about having the balance sheet balance out like a Corporate Tax Return, as you are just going off of your business earnings for the year. Decide right away whether you are going to file your taxes on a cash or accrual basis. Do you want to pay for uncollected receivables or do you want to pay for the income when it was received? You are a service company and don't have a great deal of overhead or general expenses, so filing anything different than cash wouldn't be very wise. Make sure you have closed all your year-end books by posting all business cash receipts, have paid all bills due, posted all customer payments received, and reconciled all bank statements through the end of the year. Don't forget to make sure all of your business expenses used on a credit card are posted and accounted for along with the business portion of revolving interest. A lot of times, credit card purchases are missed because they seem to be thrown in a drawer. You wouldn't miss your clients would you? Run a general ledger report as you would for any client and review each of the account's data to make sure they are posted correctly. Print out a Year to Date Profit and Loss Statement and use that finalized statement to prepare your income tax return.

If you did not record your depreciation if you have assets of value to depreciate, you can take the easy way out by using your tax software to calculate depreciation of your business assets. You are legally able to take advantage of the Section 179 Election that allows you to fully depreciate assets up to $24,000 ($100,000 for the next few years until the IRS feels they gave you enough of a break). The amount does increase over time, so keep yourself up to date on the current limit. You are not, however, allowed to fully depreciate luxury autos unless they are heavy trucks that weigh over 6,000 lbs. They'll catch on to the Hummer soon. So keep this rule in mind if you are writing off a vehicle and having your business expense the loan interest. Your depreciation deduction for vehicles isn't that grand anymore so be careful about what you think is a good buy for tax breaks. With the Section 179 allowance in mind, you can pick and choose what you want to fully depreciate, or keep depreciating for the life of the asset. It helps for creative tax accounting, especially if you have a substantial tax liability at the end of the year and need an additional writeoff. Be careful, though! Make sure you evaluate all tax liabilities while preparing your returns. If you went out and bought a new computer, software and office furniture, spending $10,000, depending on your profit you may only need to fully depreciate $5,000 to give your tax liability a break. You would then have that extra $5,000 to write off over the next four years, helping you with your tax liability for those years because you most likely won't need to go out and buy more business assets to operate. If you wrote the entire amount off and didn't need to, you would be stuck with getting nothing the following years.

Don't forget to use the "Home Office" deduction. Because you're not paying rent at a retail site, the IRS is nice enough to let you write off the portion of your home used for business. They do like to audit home business use quite a bit, so be realistic when using this deduction. If you have a mortgage on your home, then unfortunately the mortgage interest will be split into two places on your tax return – one being on your Schedule A (Itemized Deductions) and the other on your Schedule C. The IRS isn't going to allow you to take the full Mortgage Interest deduction or Property Taxes on you itemized deduction because a portion of that expense is now being transferred to your business expense. Your tax software will automatically do the transfer once you enter the data in. Unless you have an alternate utility box in your business name going to your house, your Electric, Water and Trash expenses should not be entered or paid for through your business or included in your profit and loss. These deductions will be accounted for on your Home Office use worksheet when preparing your tax returns. You can use this form to enter your Homeowners Insurance, Maintenance or direct upgrades made to your home for the purpose of your home office. Your phone bill, however, is a direct business expense, so don't worry about questioning that. If you have a DSL service that is linked to your home cable or phone and you use it for business as well, you can deduct the percent that you use for business. This deduction would be like your phone expense and your business could pay for that portion.

✓ **Preparing Client Taxes**

Tax time is a very stressful time of year. Be prepared for the long hours and time away from family fun if you intend on adding this service to your list. Most people who prepare taxes have enough clients to keep them busy with tax returns, so that is all they do. When you add bookkeeping to the mix you are going to be one very busy individual. Not only will you have to close out tax years for a handful of clients, you will have to continue to do the monthly or weekly bookkeeping for that client that you originally signed on to do. It is very easy to get behind and then projects fall through the cracks. It's not very service-oriented to put clients' bookkeeping off for a month because you were trying to fit 25 tax returns into the mix. This is where you will end up working until midnight trying to catch up. I am not trying to pop any bubbles, I am just letting you know reality. It can be done, I did it for 10 years. I still have a hard time saying no to some clients when they want me to do their tax returns. I like to be the solution for their problems, but I also know that I have a life too, and I don't want tax time to take it away from me. Find an associate who is like you, get a non-compete clause signed, and have them available in case you need help with an overload. You can also call a Temp Agency and find Tax Preparers to come in and help at tax time. You'll find out that your clients will only want you working on their accounting because they've built the trust with you, not someone else. If you hire a temp or an associate to help, REVIEW EVERYTHING THEY TOUCH! Nobody knows your job and your clients better than you, and you don't want to give your client anything that is incorrect. Have your own internal controls to make sure you are on top of every piece of paper that leaves your office.

Not all states require you to become a Licensed Tax Preparer; however, for professional and legal issues, if your state has a license available, take it. Once you have completed the state requirements to become a Licensed Tax Preparer, you must file with the state to receive your license. Check with your local state agency on filing instructions. H&R Block will provide you with this information once you complete their course. You must renew your license every year or it will expire. Each state will generally require 20 hours of qualified CPE courses to renew your license. You must submit your CPE certificate with your renewal application showing that you have completed 20 hours of required tax course training to receive your new license. Licensed Tax Preparers, Enrolled Agents, and CPAs are required to carry Bond Insurance. This is for your protection as well as your clients. You can go to almost any insurance agency such as Allstate or State Farm to purchase this policy. It generally costs around $50 for three years and you are bonded up to $10,000.

Once you become a Tax Preparer, you will receive solicitations in the mail from a number of tax-related businesses. I would renew my license by taking my 20 hours CPE through the mail from a company called Krusemarks Tax Course. They would send me updated tax information along with a test and study guide. I would study the new laws, complete the exam, and send it back to Krusemarks to grade. You must score at least a 70% to pass the test, which is not difficult. Once the tests have been graded and you pass, they will send you a certificate for your 20 hours of CPE time completed. California accepts this certificate; however check with your state agency to see if they accept it. Some states may not accept a certificate that is provided through the mail. You can also gain CPE credits through Intuit® when you become a Certified or Pro Advisor. Their CPE credits are 5 credits per test. Every year when Intuit® comes out with their upgraded software, you must renew your Certification, which includes taking their tests, so that is another resource for getting additional CPE credits.

When you initially take a tax course through H&R Block, if you score high on their final they will approach you with a job offer to prepare tax returns for the upcoming tax season. If you want the additional experience, it could possibly be a good opportunity; however, I do not recommend it. You must sign an agreement that you will not prepare tax returns on your own, but only at their tax locations. If your goal is to have your own business, then keep it that way!

The going rate for preparing a tax return depends on the complexity of the return, and the number of forms you are preparing. Generally if you are preparing a "crayon" form (1040ez), you really shouldn't charge more than $65 to prepare that return. If the return has more complexity to it, with a number of additional forms to include, you can estimate that the initial return is $65 plus $20 for each additional page. So if you're preparing a 1040 with itemized deductions, dividends, childcare expenses, earned income credit and the state forms, you should charge $165 ($65 for the federal, and $20 each for the extra five forms). If you are preparing a Schedule C (business return) you should charge an additional $100 just for the Schedule C. They are more in-depth and take longer to double-check. An appropriate price for all of the forms listed above would be $265. That is a reasonable rate.

Selecting Software to Prepare Your Tax Returns

Initially, the best way to learn how to prepare taxes from computer software is obviously TurboTax®. This software is for personal use only, and would be best used to learn how to prepare taxes, rather than to prepare multiple tax returns, without having a licensing infringement. For multiple tax return preparation, I suggest Lacert® from Intuit®. You can order it online at http://www.intuit.com/products_services/financial_prof/. You can learn more about the usage information on this software from Intuit®. There are other tax programs out there that you can use; however, they are very expensive, and until you are generating enough revenue to support purchasing those other programs, I suggest utilizing the programs that you can work with until that time.

In this course, I am not going through detailed instructions on how to prepare taxes. Please be aware and advised while reading my suggestions, that to keep current on Federal and State tax law changes, you need to take a course. I do suggest that even if you don't want to prepare tax returns, you take a course and gain knowledge in this area, because it will benefit you and your clients regardless of whether you use it for tax returns. Your clients will have more confidence in your abilities if you have more knowledge in all areas of bookkeeping. It will be a great asset to add to your resume. If you're interested in becoming an Enrolled Agent, you can do so through the Internal Revenue Service. Log on to their website located at www.irs.ustreas.gov to obtain the requirements and testing information for this. Enrolled Agents are really only one step down from a CPA; however your rate will basically stay the same. Enrolled Agents need 160 CPE Units to apply for their license, which includes testing. They test once a year, around October, and there are classes to prepare for this test, which also give you the CPE Units required by the state for your license. The difference between a Licensed Tax Preparer, an Enrolled Agent, and a CPA is basically education. A Licensed Tax Preparer is someone who has taken and passed a state test that approves their knowledge and ability in preparing tax returns. An Enrolled Agent is a Tax Preparer who is able to represent clients during IRS Audits, does not have a CPA license or even a four-year degree, but has the equivalent in experience and has studied and passed the rigorous test to become an Enrolled Agent. A CPA (Certified Public Accountant) has a four-year degree and has passed their state's CPA exam to become fully credited and licensed. Some states may not require or have testing to become a Licensed Tax Preparer, and if yours does not, make sure you take educational classes and are bonded (insured) anyway because of the liability. Regardless of whether the IRS and State holds your clients accountable for incorrect tax returns, your clients can still sue you for misrepresentation and false advice.

If you have intentions eventually of becoming a CPA, there are many requirements that you must fulfill.

- You must have a Bachelors in Accounting.
- You must complete 2 years employment at a CPA firm.
- You must test through the State Government Office.
- Once you pass the rigorous test, you can now charge $150 to $250 per hour!

If you have a client that is getting audited and you prepared the Tax Return, you can discuss the return and Financial Reports with the Agent if your client fills out an IRS Power of Attorney Form. You can also use this form to discuss Payroll Tax issues with the IRS and State Agencies as well. They will not speak to you unless otherwise noted and signed by your client. I have included the form in the CD. You cannot however be present at a trial and represent your client unless you are an Enrolled Agent or CPA. Call your favorite CPA and have them join the team. Audits are ugly and stressful for the client, and it is one great big exercise in proving a theory. You need to keep your client's records in impeccable order. Files must be organized by year, account, vendor and customer. Everything needs to have a reason, and that reason is always a document, whether it's a bank statement, canceled check, customer invoice, vendor bill, or cash receipt. Asset folders need to be made readily available. Mileage logs, travel expenses and meal expenses need to have point-of-contacts listed in order for the IRS to allow the deduction. If your client is a Corporation, all corresponding journal entries must have backup documentation explaining their purpose. The balance sheet on a Corporate Return must be justified with all bank statements, petty cash registers, Accounts Receivable Registers, Loan Documents, and especially Owner Distributions. Every year the data within the file boxes or filing cabinets need to match what is filed on their Tax Returns. If your client has a lot of cash, there needs to be a perfect tracking record on where it came from. If the IRS looks at your client's personal and business bank statements and sees all of the inflows and outflows, there needs to be justification. They will see if the total money deposited into all accounts, whether personal or business, is the same as the Net Profit, Distributions and Salaries taken by your client. If your client paid $15,000 for a truck, and the IRS couldn't match it with the revenue received throughout the year, they're going to question where the money came from. Some people are more comfortable putting cash in a safe at their house because we all know not even FDIC Insured isn't going to cover us. So if your client takes cash out in a distribution or out of his salary check when he goes to the bank, he needs to document it on a paper register and put it in his safe. Another good proving theory for cash is photographs. It's a bit difficult for the IRS to disprove Joe's claim that he took a cash withdrawal of $1,000 every month and put it into a safe, when he notes it on his check and register and takes a picture. Make sure you can prove everything so your client doesn't get into trouble.

Estimating Client Taxes

If you plan on preparing your client's personal and business tax returns, you will also need to estimate their income tax for the current fiscal year. If you have a CPA preparing the tax returns, the CPA will generally estimate the tax liability for the client. I generally charge my standard accounting hourly fee to estimate tax liabilities. Estimating is really just looking inside your crystal ball and guessing what the business is going to earn, spend, and profit in a twelve-month period. I normally estimate upon preparing a client's tax returns or reviewing their prepared returns from a CPA. Even if the CPA estimates their annualized earnings, I always double-check the CPA just in case. But that's because I do everything. . . . Throughout the fiscal year, mainly each quarter, I will analyze the income, expenses and profit so I always have the upper hand and opportunity to have the client change their estimated tax payment if necessary. Your clients will blame you if your estimating is off. No one likes a big tax bill. That is why it is very important to estimate throughout the year so there aren't any surprises. The easiest way to estimate a client's tax liability is to invest in the proper software (which you most likely have purchased already). TurboTax® is an excellent tool if you can't afford to go out and purchase Lacert®. Keep in mind, if you do use

TurboTax®, it is not intended for professionally prepared tax returns, which means that Intuit® can come after you for licensing infringement. To estimate the client's tax liability, the best place to start is with a twelve-month average. If they are a new business it is more difficult to guess what their sales are going to be, so you need to do monthly averages. The IRS and most states won't penalize a new business for underpayment of taxes in their first year. They give you a one-time allowance to get with the program and figure it out. So every three months, print out a completed quarterly profit and loss statement along with a year-to-date profit and loss. Take the numbers you see in front of you and enter them into TurboTax® as if you were preparing a return. If you are in the second quarter of the year and aren't sure what to enter for the last two quarters of the year, average out the first 6 months and use those numbers for the remainder of the fiscal year. Example:

	Jan	Feb	Mar	Apr	May	June	Total
Gross Income:	3,500	1,750	2,225	2,750	3,495	4,500	18,220
COG's:	750	225	500	600	695	800	3,570
Gross Profit:	2,750	1,495	1,725	2,150	2,800	3,700	14,650
Expenses:	600	350	700	225	995	450	3,320
Net Profit:	2,150	1,195	1,025	1,925	1,805	3,250	11,330

Look at the TOTAL net profit of $11,330. That is over a six-month period. You can average their monthly profit by taking $11,330 and dividing it by 6 months. Your client would average a Net Profit of $1,888 each month. You would then take $1,888 and multiply it by twelve months to come up with an annual estimated profit of $22,656. This is why it's important to review the profit margin every quarter. Their income could have a dramatic change and you could be caught with trying to explain to your clients why they owe more than you originally thought. Keep in mind, estimating tax liability is not just figuring what their business profit it going to be for the year. You also need to take into consideration the client's personal deductions, itemized deductions as wells as investments. The only way to get a true picture of a new client is to obtain a copy of their prior-year income tax return so that you have something to base your estimated opinion on. Otherwise you really don't know anything about their personal assets.

Estimating Corporate Tax Returns is a much bigger job. If you intend to prepare Corporate Tax Returns, make sure you have a good teacher and some experience behind you. They are a brain-melt at times, especially when the balance sheet isn't zeroing out. There are so many different rules and regulations in Corporate Taxation, that it is best to have a CPA or Enrolled Agent prepare Corporate Returns. My biggest suggestion to my clients, which I cannot stress enough, is that it is not a "good" thing if they get a refund back at the end of the tax year. No, they actually did badly. They "gave" their money to the IRS to use at their leisure all year long without getting any interest or benefits from handing out their checkbook for the government to use. But if you don't pay in enough throughout the year, the IRS penalizes you to their heart's content. It's a double standard; so I choose to estimate for my clients in such a way that they break even or are due a one-to-two percent refund after all is said and done. At least this way it's an incentive for your client to try and set up an investment account, savings account or some type of retirement account with the "Refund Money" that they would otherwise get a year later without any interest. Sounds pretty stupid to give your money to someone for free, doesn't it? As long as you estimate throughout each quarter and really focus your numbers on the third and fourth quarter, if there is a dramatic change in their profit, you can change their estimated tax coupons so they pay in enough without ending up owing a big chunk of change. Instead of being the villain, you will be the hero.

Depreciation

I have enclosed the following tables based on IRS regulations for Depreciation. They are located at the back of this book after the Index and Glossary. You can also download the Adobe pdf file at http://www.irs.gov. If you are purchasing the e-book version of this instruction guide, you will need to download the MACRS Depreciation schedule at the above-stated link, print it out and file it in a binder. If you are not familiar with depreciation and amortization, I highly suggest that you take a course on this as well. You will actually get a depreciation overview if you enroll in the H&R Block Tax School. There are so many different areas of depreciation that are covered, you really need to understand the fundamentals of a fixed asset.

The general rule of depreciation, as a quick guide, is taking the purchase price of an asset and writing off a portion of that dollar amount over the given recovery life of an asset. Your asset life is listed broken down by classification on your Instruction From 4562 from the IRS.

> Example: If you have a computer that you purchased for $2,000 in January of a given year, the IRS asset life is 5 years; you would take $2,000 divided by 5, which is $400. That is your <u>annual</u> depreciation.

If you have a client who is on an accrual basis, or one that is a Corporation, you would need to depreciate each asset on a monthly basis to show your actual balances on your fixed assets. It also effects your Profit and Loss statement with a more accurate summary of booked expenses. Your monthly depreciation for the computer would be $33.33, adjusting the 12th-month journal entry to reflect the difference of four cents to equal $400.

Your journal entry would look like this for a monthly depreciation:

01/31/08   0108-001JM (JM lets me know I created the journal entry)

Account	Debit	Credit	
1407	$33.33		Record January 2008 computer depreciation
1151		$33.33	Record January 2008 accumulated depreciation

Depreciation is actually rather easy; just familiarize yourself with an "asset life" of that particular fixed asset and MACRS. **Special Note** Remember that if you have an asset placed in service on any other given month besides January, you will have to use the percentage ratio for Mid-Quarter, Half-Quarter, 3rd Quarter, so you don't depreciate a full year that isn't allowed because of the date of purchase for the asset. There are other depreciation methods used for the IRS and State regulations; these depend entirely on the type of asset and when it was placed in service. You can download the ACRS (Accelerated Depreciation) schedule from the IRS website for more rules and regulations.

Chapter 6
Common Questions

✓ Educational Requirements

Many of you have asked me if I thought that having a degree was required for you to have your own bookkeeping or accounting business. Some were very concerned that they did not, and that this would hinder their ability to get clients. I try not to be so blunt with my opinion, but my job is to honestly answer your questions, giving you a blue-collar opinion on business. How important is a business degree in accounting? An educational piece of paper is mandatory if your intentions are working for someone else. An education is important for teaching you the basic fundamentals of accounting; however, the majority of you buying this book come from on-the-job training as a bookkeeper, an Accounts Payable or Receivable clerk, or from a field in relation to accounting. You have worked your way up the chain of command, learning as you go. Many of you do not have a 4-year degree. Do you know what you're doing? Do you understand Assets, Liabilities, Invoicing and Paying Bills? I am a firm believer that on-the-job training is more valuable than a degree. The only person it is not valuable to is someone trying to get a job at Xerox Corporation as the Controller or CFO. Then, I can assure you, your experience will not matter if you don't have a degree. They want a piece of paper that confirms the fact that you were taught the politically correct way of working for someone else. If you eventually want to become a CPA, then it is required that you have a 4-year accounting degree. My company makes its own requirements because it's mine! Do you think that I don't know what I'm talking about? Do my books give any indication of my inability or length of education? Well guess what, I myself do not have my accounting degree, either. I do have over 14 years of on-the-job training. I've taken classes on subject areas that I need in order to get my CPE credits for my tax license, and I have been hired by several companies in San Diego to train their employees, set up their accounting departments and streamline the structure with the employees who have graduated with a BS in Accounting, and the sad truth is, their inexperience was so definite that the accounting degree didn't mean a thing. The small business world doesn't revolve around widgets, and when someone who has spent in excess of $100,000 on an education in accounting doesn't know how to set up a balance sheet, there is a serious problem. I don't know who the smarter one is. I had a debate with a CPA's employee a few years ago. I can do just about everything a CPA does; there are some things that I can't do and don't know, but I do know where to find out. The CPA's employee just passed his CPA exam after the State of California required two years of working for a CPA firm and a four-year degree, and he thought he was better than I was because of that piece of paper. In those six years he had been going to school and paid over $100,000, while working for a CPA firm at $15 per hour. In six years I had earned over $350,000 working for myself, and I still know more than he does. So you tell me, do you think you won't make it if you don't have that piece of paper? I don't! I do think that a college degree is important, and if you have yours it is just more confirmation that you were trained through school, but I don't think that you need to have one to be successful. Sometimes I do wish I had finished college just to say that I did, but then I do look at what I have accomplished and I'm okay with it. I frankly don't want to be a CPA; I'm finishing my studies for a CFE (Certified Fraud Examiner), and I am able to sit for the CFE exam because of my experience – which I am grateful for, because Financial Fraud is what I rather enjoy doing. But owning a bookkeeping service and taking care of small businesses doesn't require you to be college-educated. On-the-job training is okay.

Age and experience relate to another problem that I see happening with people who are trying their employment options. If you are over 50 and trying to find a job, interviews are intimidating if you are insecure about your age. Though we may like to believe that the world doesn't discriminate, well, think again. It does. There will be 100 reasons why you didn't get a job when you had more experience and credentials than someone else 20 years younger who applied for the same job. Of course the employer can't ever admit to that, but they are looking out for the best interest of their company, even if it means not hiring someone older. Enter self-employment. You take a 50-year-old self-employed accountant or bookkeeper, and you are going to have small business owners confident in your experience rather than using it against you. If you are starting out on your own after you have worked for someone else for 30 years, then use it to your advantage, because it won't matter with the tables turned. They need you, which is why they're looking. I do get questioned about my experience, and not because of my age, but my appearance. I should be flattered that I get carded for lottery tickets. Mine is a constant struggle to prove to clients that I know what I'm doing. If they are a referral, it's a lot easier because someone already told them I was good. But if I have an appointment with a new client and it is cold turkey, the look on their face is always classic. I just apparently look really young for my age. One time, I actually couldn't resist with my wit and humor to give one back. I couldn't help but notice how much my client's assistant was staring at me at our first meeting. The look on his face was not rude, but questioning. I knew right away that he was wondering if I was even 20. I looked at him and said "Oil of Olay works wonders; I'm actually a lot older than you are thinking right now." I am over 30, and I'll just leave it at that. I have found a few gray hairs, but nothing a good visit to the salon can't fix!

✓ **Experience**

Being the new name on the block is so hard, especially when you're not sure of what to tell a client when they ask how much experience you have as a new business. The bottom line is, even if your business is two months new and you have been doing bookkeeping or accounting for five years, you have five years of experience. Never forget that. Your business may be new, but your experience is not. Get a letter of recommendation from your prior bosses if possible. If you left on good terms, and never got that letter of recommendation, give them a call and ask them for one. You can include your recommendation letters on your web page or in your promotional package, even if it isn't the full letter and you type in a partial blurp of what they said. Small businesses have more confidence in you when you are experienced.

If you lack a great deal of bookkeeping experience and you are buying this book for a change of career, I not only highly recommend that you buy *I have QuickBooks, Now What*, but also begin by limiting your services. An inexperienced bookkeeper needs to understand how to set up QuickBooks®, and how to create a Chart of Accounts, balance sheet, and profit and loss statement. This is where you would focus your skills on what you already know. Most of you pay your bills at home, reconcile your bank statements, and keep on top of the basic bookkeeping. Have your networking CPA do month-end financials until you understand and are more comfortable with what you are creating. There are plenty of businesses out there who need someone like you to come in once a week, cut checks, invoice clients, and reconcile the bank accounts so they know how much money they have. You need to start somewhere, and that is the best place. The liability isn't as high if you make mistakes because you will also have a CPA or accountant reviewing your work. There is also a school in Utah called Universal Accounting. They offer a course for people wanting to learn bookkeeping and accounting, and with the course they also offer a specific course on opening your own bookkeeping business as well. The course is around $1,600, which they bill you for at $149 a month for 18 months. I have included a coupon with this book for the Universal Accounting program course. I have heard from students who have taken their course and also purchased my books that their accounting course is an excellent resource for accounting education. Once you pass their test at the end of the course, you become designated as a "Professional Bookkeeper" and can include the "PB" designation after your title.

Another excellent resource, especially to become a Certified Bookkeeper, is the American Institute of Professional Bookkeepers. When you become a member and pass their bookkeeping test, you are given a certificate and can use the CB (Certified Bookkeeper) after your title. The membership is normally $60 per year, for which you receive newsletters and special member discounts, plus they offer an exclusive free telephone answer line if you have questions. Their contact information is also in the back of this book.

✓ **Sales**

I have been asked many times why I don't focus on the sales process of cold calls, letters or going door to door. One woman was incredibly concerned because she was new to her area and didn't know anyone. Everybody is new and just starting out, meaning that it doesn't matter if you are new to the area or not; the Networking individuals listed in my book are the key resource in getting those referrals, no matter whether you are new to an area or not. When I started, I didn't use people that I currently knew such as family, friends and acquaintances, because they are not the specific industry referrals you need for accounting and bookkeeping. I can guarantee you, though, if you are new to an area, using just a sales letter it will be extremely hard to get your foot in the door. You are more likely to be "trusted" by a potential client if someone told them about you. There are a few topics that I may sound like a broken record on, and yes, this is one of them. Finances and money are a very personal subject matter that often makes people a bit paranoid. It takes a great deal of trust and naivety on your client's part to call a potential accountant or bookkeeper cold turkey from a phone book or from a sales letter that they may receive in the mail. Isn't it a thousand times easier and less stressful to just pick up the phone and ask Chris at Paychex whom they would recommend to others? Think of the tables being reversed. Are you going to call any contractor out of the phone book or are you going to ask your neighbor, even if you are new to the area, if they know of any good contractors? This by any means isn't to say, don't do any sales; it just means that the majority of your clients are going to come from referrals. If you want to do sales and have at least two prior employers who will type you up a letter of recommendation, then include them with your promo package, on your website or on a list of a references for someone to call and ask if you are trustworthy and any good at what you do.

✓ **Competition**

Competition is the hardest part of any business. If you look in your local Yellow Pages, you will see pages of bookkeeping and accounting services. You will then start to question how you can possibly compete with so many. The difference between you and them is going to be your networking group. There are millions of businesses and over 75% of them are small businesses. More and more people are tired of working for someone else, just like you. They are afraid of layoffs, downsizing and corporate politics, so they take their skill or trade and go at it on their own. The small business sector is the specialty you should focus on. There is plenty of work to go around; however, just winging it on your own without knowing what do to and where to find clients will be your failure. You not only have to have the best resource for referrals, which now you will, you will also have to offer something the bookkeeping service down the street does not. Service, Solutions, Quality and Reliability. Almost every small business that is already up and running has someone who is doing their books. But are they doing a good job, are they dependable and reliable, and do they prepare professional reports and quality work? Never talk down about any other bookkeeping businesses out there. No one likes to hear negativity and gossip, and it will classify you in a certain reference to other companies. If you are approached to take over from another bookkeeping service and you do a much better job than the previous bookkeeper, your client will know it just by seeing what you are doing. They don't want you to criticize them for hiring the wrong bookkeeper. They make management mistakes as well. If they ask you "how things look," meaning their books, and they are a mess, you can say that the books were not maintained but you're cleaning them up to perfection. You don't want to say, "What were you thinking! The previous bookkeeper didn't know what she was doing!" If you are serious and up for the battle, the next year when the Yellow Pages come out again there will be someone like you looking at your bookkeeping business wondering how I am going to compete!

✓ Mistakes to Avoid

If you're not licensed or in the process of becoming licensed as a Tax Preparer, CPA or Enrolled Agent, do not complete business or personal tax returns yourself unless it is your own. The liability is too high if you incorrectly prepare a return. You could be held accountable through all of the tax agencies, not to mention getting sued by your clients. A CPA firm can bring you more business in return if you handle all of the bookkeeping and general accounting needs of their clients; thus you should bring the tax returns to the CPAs. Some states do not require you to be licensed to prepare income tax returns; however, tax laws are ever changing, and if you want to do taxes, just to have certification, get licensed. Clients also appreciate the fact that a CPA can target a wider range of tax breaks and really justify their fees by reducing a client's tax liability to the utmost possible. I have a client who went to a hole-in-the wall Tax Preparer, and every year he would owe the IRS at least $14,000. I brought in my "favorite" CPA and told him that the tax returns were wrong and we needed to file an amended return. My client not only got a $10,000 refund from his prior two years' tax returns, but his current-year tax liability, with just about the same Net Profit, was only $5,000 because of missed deductions. When you owe $5,000 rather than $14,000, don't you think you would be a bit happy with the results, even if the bill was a few hundred dollars more?

NEVER, NEVER, NEVER, go to work for <u>any</u> of your clients as an "employee," no matter how enticing the job offer sounds!!! It will ruin your business relationship immediately. You lose all confidence you created for yourself being self-employed, and most of all, you lose all freedom you created for yourself being self-employed. Short story: I had a client that was a "Laboratory." I set up the accounting department when the corporation first opened its doors. I had a highly respectable business relationship with my client. The President offered me a job. CFO sounded too good to turn down. Three years I had spent building my business to success. With the birth of my second daughter I hadn't time to really "think" about what I had done by taking that job offer. I sold all of my clients, and thought that I had made the "right decision." The <u>second</u> I walked in the front door of that business I knew it was the worst mistake I ever made. Everything changed; my "boss" was completely opposite the way she appeared as my client. I was constantly backed into a corner. My boss no longer took my advice as a professional, but now ridiculed me as an "employee." It took me five months to finally say I had enough. I went into her office with my letter of resignation, and told her that I could not be an "employee." It is not in my personality. Within the instant that I resigned, my confidence came back, and she could no longer "tell" me what to do or say. I had all of the control back for myself. I made five phone calls that day to past contacts that had brought me business, and within three weeks, I had landed three new clients, and incidentally, kept the old client that I went to work for because she begged me to stay as their "contracted accountant."

If you don't know how to do something, know where to go to find the resources to learn it!! Everything you do will be a learning experience for you. If a client has a question that you don't know the answer to, there is nothing wrong with admitting it. Find out what the answer is, and call the client back as soon as possible with the results.

If you made a mistake, admit to it and rectify it immediately!

Be reliable and dependable. If you change an appointment because of a family emergency, such as your children being sick, your clients will understand. Always tell them when you will be able to reschedule.

If you hire someone to work for you doing books for your clients, make sure you make a contract between you and the employee in reference to your clients. Also make them aware that they work for you, and it is not a partnership. A lot of times, especially small companies have difficulties explaining to employees that they are not part owner. Never make that mistake. You'll lose in court if you're not absolutely clear with them.

If you are not a Licensed CPA, you cannot use the word "Accountant" or "Accounting" in your <u>Company</u> name without stating that you are a "Non" CPA Firm. If you do, some State Board of Accountancies will revoke your business license and fine you up to $2,500 for appropriation or misuse of name. It is considered misleading, that you are in direction violation of and competing with the qualifications of a Certified Public Accountant. Check with your state Accounting Board for their rules and regulations. My company's legal name is San Diego Business Accounting Solutions, a "Non" CPA Firm.

A key indication about networking contacts who refer bad clients: if there are more than three clients referred to you by one particular networking referral, CPA, or payroll company, who don't pay or are extremely slow to pay, this will indicate the type of clients this contact works with. For your sanity and efforts, politely turn down any more referrals from them. It will get very costly and difficult budgeting around someone who isn't paying. You'll just end up losing time and money.

Getting burned out . . . it happens to all of us. I've become burned out many times. If you are ever feeling the burnout of self-employment, do yourself a favor and take a break. The hardest part of being your own boss is the constant reminder that you don't get vacation pay. You still need a vacation. Your brain needs to take a break too, and if you don't treat it, you will get burned out by your third year. It is hard work, especially knowing you are responsible for making that dollar. Someone else's company isn't cutting you a paycheck every week, so what you do with your business is your responsibility. Even if you close down your office for three days – five would be best, but three will do you a bit of good. Budget it in for yourself as your goal because I promise you, you will need it. It doesn't mean you need to spend $5,000 going to London. Just don't go to work. Don't answer the phone, and don't pick up your mail at the P.O. Box. Change your voice mail, contact your clients the week before and let them know you will be out of town. It doesn't matter how far out of town you go. You could take your kids or spouse to a movie and consider that your vacation. Go shopping, or do whatever hobby you enjoy doing, but give yourself a break. You will work so much better when you return, and when you're feeling overloaded again, plan a three-day weekend. You are entitled to take care of yourself.

Another suggestion, and with this politically correct world I'm taking a risk in even voicing my option, but what the heck. Stress can get the best of us! My plate still gets so full that I think I'm going to go over the deep end. I do not believe in medicating people with drugs that cause so many side effects that before you know it, instead of the heart failing, it will just blow up! Did you know that exercise, especially cardiovascular exercise, releases natural serotonin in your brain? That's the same thing the research labs are trying to put into Prozac® and Zoloft®. Exercising not only reduces stress, but the side effects are energy, weight loss or maintenance, normal sleeping patterns, calmness in stressful situations, and it creates a great sense of self-esteem. Compare these with cottonmouth, problems sleeping, increased heart rate, heart failure, high blood pressure, nausea and sexual problems. Take your pick of side effects; I choose to run because I'm not getting any younger, and I don't want a medicine cabinet filled with prescriptions that cost more than a mortgage payment every month. It relieves my stress and makes me feel good. I have days where I have to kick myself to go running because I just don't feel like it, but when I'm done I feel like I just conquered a mountain. The best part about running for me is that I run outside. I schedule myself everyday before I pick up my girls, and when you run outside, you don't have any excuses not to finish, because you have to get back! There is no possibility of hitting the stop button on the treadmill when you are two miles away from your car. If you don't exercise, try it, even if you go for long walks.

✓ Problem Clients

The problem client; I wish I could say that you won't have any, but then I would be lying. It doesn't matter what industry you're in, there will be times that you have to deal with clients who are demanding, don't pay, and sometimes even worse. Most of your clients will be appreciative and happy with you if you do a good job. But be prepared just in case you get one bad one.

If you don't like a client and they are too unbearable to work with, refer them to someone else. The best way to handle it, is to first tell an associate (CPA or another Bookkeeping Service) that you have a client that you don't have time for, tell them what the client's annoying points are, and see if they want to take over. Then tell the client that on such and such a date, CPA Joe will be taking over for you because you are too overloaded with work. Don't ever say it's because they're too unbearable to work with.

Never leave an account incomplete. If you drop a client because of their personality or any other reason, always finish your job no matter how difficult they are. If you tell them you will have someone else come in on Oct 1st, then you finish your work up until Sept 30th. Nine out of ten times, that client, even though they are difficult, will think you're the greatest thing and refer you to someone else down the road. It's happened to me several times.

Don't except any work or deadlines from a client who is behind on their bills. Always make them pay their past due balances before you begin more work. Do what you can to be polite about it, but also don't back yourself into a corner; you have expenses, too.

If you have a client who isn't paying, or whom you know you won't collect money from, but you have completed their work, <u>Do Not</u> give them any financial reports that you have completed. There is a fine line of legality about whether you can withhold their data that they supplied to you such as receipts, checkbook registers and bank statements. Whether my way is the correct way or not, this is the way I handle it; you of course can use your own best judgment. I have this little rule when clients go beyond their payment point. If four months go by and you have tried to collect on an invoice for completed work, their files automatically go into storage. Funny, I can't seem to go get their paperwork out of storage because now the storage bill is $25 multiplied by however many months it was there. "I'd be happy to get you your files, but first you must bring a certified check or cash for the storage, plus the balance of the invoice." They can take you to court over it, and if the circumstances are urgent for those files, request the attorney to pay the storage bill to get them out. You may never see payment on your invoice, but it sure is difficult to get boxes from storage when there is a balance due. They can't force you to pay more fees for a deadbeat client. If they want it, let them pay to get it out. You can already consider them gone, and you wouldn't want to do any more work for them anyway. Be polite about it, but also remember that you did work for them and are entitled to get paid. Always have the upper hand. Consider the option that there will be a stop-payment on your check as well, so a cashier's check or money order will be the only form of payment. If they refuse to pay, they're going to have a difficult time filing their taxes or recreating books without proper records. They can always get another copy of their bank statement, but without canceled checks, you'd be amazed how hard it is to prove to the IRS what a particular expense was justified for.

Will the messenger ever get killed? As a matter of fact, yes. There are going to be times when you get yelled at, get the cold shoulder or even threatened. Remember how I mentioned that I don't like to do taxes anymore – it's because of this issue. You can estimate your client's tax liability the entire year until you're blue in the face, but that doesn't mean that they're actually going to pay that estimated tax payment on the due date. Then at the beginning of the year when you're finalizing their tax returns and they owe $20,000, they're going to get upset. You, being the only one responsible because you prepared it, will take the brunt. It doesn't matter that they bought a Hummer or a Sub-Zero and remodeled their house. That doesn't ever come into consideration when they owe the IRS. Anytime a client gets a notice in the mail from any tax agency, you will be the first person they call to ask why. The assumption is that you made a mistake, but the reality is they didn't fulfill their responsibility as a business owner. Just last week, ironically enough, I had the joyous job of telling two clients that their checking accounts were upside down because their bookkeeper wasn't posting the payroll tax payments from the Paychex payroll reports. One client was upside down $28,000 and the other one was negative $12,000. It's never an easy job, but you have to do it. Their face might turn red, but what I always tell them is, "Wouldn't you rather know"? That's what they hired you for, whether it's good news or bad news, so you must be prepared to be killed. It's all in how you handle it. There is only so much you can do to please people, and if 99% of the year they have good news, that 1% is still uncomfortable; but that is life. Take it with a grain of salt, be professional, listen and have solutions for them if possible, but never get angry back. It won't ever solve anything. Keep in mind a few good rules of self-employment with small businesses and you'll be fine. First rule is, clients don't understand or comprehend the tax laws. Second rule, they aren't good with budgeting their money, which makes for a very bad combination when tax time comes around. I take absolute pride in the fact that I can estimate my client's taxes for the upcoming year and come within 1% of their tax liability without purging or messing with the numbers. It is a very difficult and daunting task because you have to look within your crystal ball and guess what their business is going to do. I give constant reminders of what they need to pay in when the quarterly tax payments are due, so they are not taken by surprise. I re-estimate their taxes every quarter by reviewing my assumption vs. their actual figures and seeing what the difference is. If there is a significant change in their income, I re-issue new estimated coupons for the remainder of the year. They never like it when I give them the new payment coupons, but they like it a lot less when they owe $20,000.

I'll give you one horror story just because. Not that I want to scare you off, but I want you to be aware of a changing personality with some clients. One bad seed isn't going to affect your business if you ever happen to get one like this. A few years ago I had a client who was a cigarette manufacturer (I don't smoke, go figure). I got along great with the accountant and at the time the CEO. The CEO ended up opening a cigarette store and asked me to set up the books. So of course I did. His records were a mess, his employees stole money and he liked to hide cash. When I set up the store, I sent over a contract such as the one in this book, stating all the services that I would provide for his store. He specifically told me that he did not want me to prepare his Sales Tax Returns, that he would do it himself. We all know why, because he's hiding cash. He started to nickel and dime me and would sit on my invoices for over 60 days. So I refused to do any more work for him until he caught up. I had his records, bank statements, cash receipts and checks for the prior few months and would not release them until he caught up on his bills, nor did I complete the accounting for them because I was not getting paid. One day he received a notice of intent to revoke the store's sales tax license form the State Board for failure to submit and pay his sales taxes. He called me up immediately and chewed me out. I reminded him of the contract that he'd signed, stating that he was to process his own sales tax, as per his request. He cussed me out and told me, "Just get it done," then abruptly hung up on me. I called him back, got his voice mail of course and left him a message telling him I'd be glad to prepare them for him, but first he needed to pay me. He sent the accountant from the other company over to my office to pick up all his files. He didn't have a check with him so I refused to give them to him. They were in storage. I told the accountant that I was resigning as his accountant and that no further services would be completed for the store because of the vulgarity and bad treatment. So this client calls and leaves another message stating that he spoke with his attorney, and I would have to prepare everything for him because I knew he would eventually pay me. So I called my attorney and asked him to call this client and tell him, in a professional way, to shove it. After these phone games, I got a phone call immediately after my attorney called my client, and I let it go to voice mail because I didn't want to talk to him any longer. He was actually ignorant enough to leave a message. I have it on my dictaphone to this day. It said, "You're going to need more than an attorney when I'm through with you, you better watch your back." So, for the next few months I was constantly watching my back. Nothing ever came of his threat, but I will always hold on to any piece of evidence in case something were to ever come up again. If you start to see warning signs from clients with the potential of becoming aggressive or even dangerous, do yourself a favor by resigning your services. There is no reason why you need to feel uncomfortable because of the way someone is treating you. Remember, when you own this business, the decisions are up to you.

A client wanting you to purge entries or hide cash is a big warning sign for the exit door. Prison time doesn't sound so fun when you could be held accountable for Fraud or Tax Evasion. If a client ever mentions cash payments under the table or something that you know is not correct, first and foremost, don't do it. Second, tell them you don't want to know about it. My accounting mind has always been investigative, so anytime I am preparing financials for clients and see a purchase, sale or name on the register that catches my eye – and everything catches my eye – I question it. I question it while requesting backup documentation to justify their claim. I don't nickel and dime and I'm not going to argue about a McDonalds receipt with two happy meals, but I am going to argue if there is something that is completely unjustified. My goal is to give my clients the best possible legal tax breaks. Creative accounting does not have to be illegal. A lot of small business owners don't realize that there are so many more tax laws and tax breaks that they aren't aware of, and they automatically try to find an easy way out. If you are a good bookkeeper or accountant, they will still save thousands of dollars in taxes.

✓ **Troubleshooting**

Setting up Payroll in QuickBooks Pro® to correctly post payroll liabilities; Make sure you go to your item list in QuickBooks Pro® that has all of the tax and account information in payroll. In order for your liabilities to post to the correct account, you <u>must</u> make sure that it is set up the right way. When payroll is not posted correctly, your balance sheet will show it. Try explaining to your clients why their payroll tax liability accounts are showing liability when you've already posted the payroll tax payment – it would be rather embarrassing. They will think you don't know what you're doing. Double-check your setup by reviewing the Sample Company provided in this manual. In the QuickBooks® payroll item list, just make sure that the payroll tax items accounts are tracked through the payroll liability and not payroll expense. If you are paying the payroll taxes through QuickBooks® by using the payroll feature, your tax payments won't balance out to the liability if not set up correctly.

You posted transactions to QuickBooks Pro®, but you can't find the entry and your Balance Sheet and Income Statement don't reflect what you did; In most cases, you entered your date wrong on the transaction. Normally it's the year that is not correct. Click on your "FIND" button, and enter the amount of the entry. Make sure you don't select a date range, so it searches the entire database. Once it pulls up the entries that match the transaction you entered, double-click on the entry and view the date. If that is the problem then change the date.

Your Income Statements (Profit & Loss) net income doesn't match your Balance Sheet; Generally when this happens, your fiscal year report period is incorrect. If you're running a monthly financial report from May 1st to May 31st, your Net Income on your Balance Sheet is not going to match because your Balance Sheet is calculating the entire fiscal year. Your Income Statement is only calculating the month of May. You need to run a Year to Date report showing all of the months outlined. Make sure your fiscal year is correct as well. If your client is not using the standard calendar year, your reports need to reflect that.

Purchase Orders; If your client is in the construction/service industry and they are not creating purchase orders, they could be losing thousands of dollars every year. I had a client who made cabinets. When I picked up his account, he literally had piles of unopened bills on the floor for years. He would just wait until the vendor called him to collect money. He would pay the amount that they said was overdue without question. I can guarantee that he had paid for supplies, finance charges, and invoices that were not his because he paid his bills this way. Just by creating a purchase order and using the vendor order book or price list (especially when there is a sales rep involved for discounts) you will always compare the packing slip when the materials are received to the purchase order, and then to the invoice when it is received. You would be surprised at how many errors there are on pricing for products as well as not receiving the same quantity that were billed or ordered. People are human; however, it is always a costly mistake, especially to the person not double-checking someone else's work. When you're trying to land an account, tell them that they could recover the cost of your services not only through the efficiency of your work, but by how much you could save them on billing errors as well. In essence, you're really not costing them anything additional, but you're saving them money.

Trying to obtain loan documents from independent investors; If you have a problem when you're requesting a copy of loan papers on a note that your client has received for their personal use or business that is from an individual and not a banking institution, and they are refusing to provide that documentation, you can bet it is a scam. I had a client in this exact position, and when I started requesting the loan documents to finalize the balance sheet, the "individual" kept coming up with excuses. Finally when an attorney became involved, we found out that the money my client borrowed, in the amount of $80,000, turned into a balloon payment of $500,000 plus the $80,000 in five years. They were completely ripped off. Keep your eyes open and go with your gut instinct if you feel that something just doesn't seem right.

Chapter 7

Forms

I have included the following forms that I have created throughout the years to make my business run much more smoothly. These forms are also included on your CD in pdf format. If you need to install Adobe to read these files, you can download their free pdf reader at www.adobe.com.

- Quote Sheet
- Proposal Letter
- Contract
- Client Work-Folder
- New Client Checklist
- Client Monthly Checklist (Insert this in the front of each client's 3-ring binder for your records, to check off each item so you don't forget to include any reports for your clients.)
- Client Year End Checklist (Insert this behind the client monthly checklist in your binder.)
- Client's Monthly Checklist (Give this to your client so they don't forget to give you everything you need.)
- Bank Reconciliation
- Outstanding (un-cleared) Check List
- Journal Entry Form
- WIP Report (Work in Progress)
- Collection Letters (3)
- IRS Power of Attorney (on CD only)
- Non-Compete Agreement
- Sales Letters (2)
- Depreciation Instructions Form 4562 (CD Only)

QUOTE SHEET

Date: _____   Company: _____

Contact: _____   Phone No. _____

Address: _____

Fax No: _____   Referred By: _____

Type of Business - _____

Sole Proprietor/Partnership/Corp: _____   Other: _____

Number of Employees: _____   No of Checks written: _____

Special Reports Needed: _____   Quarterly Taxes & W2's: _____

Payroll Services: _____   Sales Tax/Workers Comp: _____

Misc.: _____

ADDITIONAL SERVICES NEEDED?

Accounts Payable (How Often) -   Re-Organizing Books (How far back?)

Accounts Receivable (How Often) -   Consulting/Training -

Audit Preparation -

Monthly Rate - $_____   Reorganize - $_____

Payroll Service $_____   Consult/Training - $_____

A/P Service - $_____   Set Up Fee - $_____

A/R Service - $_____   Add't Fee - $_____

       Total Charges - $_____

COMMENTS:

(Proposal Letter)

Dear --------,

It was a pleasure meeting with you last week. Thank you for your time and for giving me the opportunity to quote on your accounting and bookkeeping needs.

By analyzing your business needs and financial goals, I believe that these are the following services that would meet your needs.

1. Weekly Accounts Payable
2. Weekly Accounts Receivable
3. Monthly Financial Reports
4. Year End Accounting

The costs associated with these services are $0.00 per hour, (or per month) my estimated time per week would be 8 hours totaling $0.00 per month.

I am looking forward to building a long lasting business relationship with you, and helping your business become more profitable.

Sincerely,

Julie A. Mucha

(Your company name and address here)

Engagement Agreement for Accounting Services

Company Name:
Address: _____

                _____

Dear Client:

This document is written to confirm our understanding of the terms of our engagement and the nature and extent of the accounting and tax services that we will provide to you.

We will prepare your (monthly/weekly/bi-weekly) accounting and bookkeeping for your company. Our work is not audited, however we will submit un-audited financial reports and statements for your records. We will be available to assist and guide you in gathering the necessary information by furnishing you with a monthly worksheet to keep track of the necessary documents that we will need.

It is your responsibility to provide all of the information necessary to complete your financial reports and tax returns. You should retain all the documents, receipts, and cancelled checks and other records to substantiate the items of income and deductible expenditures, which are claimed on your year end tax return.

Fees for our services will be at $____ per hour (or a flat rate depending on what work your generating). Additionally, we will be entitled to reimbursement for out-of-pocket expenses, which may include, but not limited to the following, long distance phone calls, and copy costs. Our preparation fees must be paid upon delivery, and in some cases a retainer may be required. We reserve the right to stop working on your account whenever billed fees are not paid when due and furthermore will not be held accountable for the late filing of any State or Federal Tax Return when services have rendered due to non-payment of your account with San Diego Business Accounting Solutions.

This engagement includes only those services specifically described in this agreement. In the unlikely event of disagreement over the payment for services, we agree now to go to small claims court or to resolutions by arbitration by the American Arbitration Association (AAA) and waive the right to litigation, other than to enforce a decision by the AAA. The prevailing party shall be entitled to reasonable collection costs and attorney's fees, according to the decision of the arbitrators.

If the foregoing is in accordance with our understanding of the terms and conditions of our engagement, please sign both copies and keep one for your records returning the second copy to us. If your accounting needs change during the year, the nature of our services can be adjusted appropriately.

We wish to express our appreciation for this opportunity to work with you and we are always available to discuss or clarify any part of this letter.

_____   _____
Your name here   Date

_____   _____
Client Name here   Date

CLIENT WORK-FOLDER

EMPLOYEE: _____   WEEK: _____

Date	CLIENT	Time In	Time Out	Scope of Work Performed	Total Hrs	Rate	Billed

New Client Checklist - Please provide the following documentation to start your accounting information. Put a check in each box for all the documenation included. If it does not apply, please mark it n/a.

Description		If not available (date expected)
Current Balance Sheet	☐	_____
Current Profit & Loss Statement	☐	_____
Automobile Notes/Information	☐	_____
Equipment Notes/Receipts	☐	_____
Loans/Documentation	☐	_____
Checkbook Register - Chkng	☐	_____
Checkbook Register - Savings	☐	_____
Checkbook Register - Payroll	☐	_____
Bank Statements - General	☐	_____
Bank Statements - Savings	☐	_____
Bank Statements - Payroll	☐	_____
Cancelled Checks	☐	_____
Daily Cash Report	☐	_____
Daily Sales Report	☐	_____
Accounts Receivable Aging	☐	_____
Accounts Payable Aging	☐	_____
Accounts Receivable Invoices	☐	_____
Accounts Payable Invoices	☐	_____
Petty Cash Report	☐	_____
Payroll Report	☐	_____
Workers Compensation Form	☐	_____
Sales Tax Form	☐	_____
Credit Card Statements	☐	_____
W9 Forms Completed	☐	_____
Misc. Cash Receipts	☐	_____
Asset List	☐	_____
Fed Tax ID No. (or S.S.N)	☐	_____
State Tax ID No. (or S.S.N)	☐	_____
	☐	_____

CLIENT: _____   **Monthly Check-List**

YEAR: _____

Description	Jan	Feb	Mar	Apr	May	June	July	Aug	Sep	Oct	Nov	Dec
Date Received												
Date Due												
Reviewed By												
Balance Sheet												
Profit & Loss												
General Ledger												
Sales Report												
A/R Aging												
A/P Aging												
Budget - Cash Flow												
1099's (W9's requested)												
Bank Recs												
Payroll Reports												
Payroll Taxes												
Sales Tax Form												
Workers Comp												

QUARTERLY REMINDERS

Financial Packages												
Sales Tax												
Estimated Tax Due												
Payroll Taxes Due												

CLIENT: _____   **YEAR END CHECKLIST**

YEAR: _____

Description	Balance Out	Completed	Adjustments	Finalized	
Balance Sheet					
Profit & Loss					
General Ledger					
Payroll & W2's					
1099's Issued					
Depreciation					
Amortization					
Prepaid Taxes					
Notes					

TAX RETURN INFORMATION

CPA FIRM: _____   DUE DATE: _____

CONTACT: _____   COMPLETED: _____

PHONE NO: _____   DELIVERY DATE: _____

SIGNED: _____

DATE: _____

CLIENTS MONTHLY CHECKLIST -   Please place a check by each box when preparing your documents for monthly financial reports. If it doesn't apply please mark n/a. (Copies are okay)

Description	Jan	Feb	Mar	Apr	May	June	July	Aug	Sep	Oct	Nov	Dec
Checkbooks Register - Chkng												
Checkbooks Register - Savings												
Checkbooks Register - Payroll												
Bank Statements - Chkng												
Bank Statements - Savings												
Bank Statements - Payroll												
Cancelled Checks												
Daily Cash Report												
Daily Sales Report												
Accounts Receivable Aging												
Accounts Payable Aging												
Petty Cash Report (receipts)												
Payroll Reports												
Workers Comp Form												
Sales Tax Form												
Credit Card Statements												
W9 Forms Completed												
Quickbooks Back-up File												

-BANK RECONCILIATION-

Company: _____

Account: _____

Month Ending: _____

Bank Balance As Of   _____ $ _____

Deposits In Transit $ _____

Less Outstanding Checks $ _____

Bank Charges $ _____

Adjustments $ _____

Bank Balance As Of   _____ $ _____

Book Balance As Of   _____ $ _____

Deposits $ _____

Disbursements: Check No. _____ to _____ $ _____

Bank Charges $ _____

Interest $ _____

Voided Checks $ _____

Adjustments $ _____

Automatic Bank Withdrawls $ _____

Book Balance As Of   _____ $ _____

Prepared By: _____   Date: _____

-OUTSTANDING CHECK LIST-

Company: _____   Account: _____

Month Ending: _____   Total $ _____

Ck No.	Amount		Ck No.	Amount		Ck No.	Amount
Total:			Total:			Total:	

Total <u>All</u> Collumns: _____

JOURNAL ENTRY FORM

JOURNAL ENTRY NO.:

COMPANY:

PERIOD ENDING: ___ / ___ / ___

DEBIT COLUMNS				CREDIT COLUMNS				
DIV	GL ACCT	AMOUNT		DIV	GL ACCT	AMOUNT		DESCRIPTION
TOTAL								

PREPARED BY: _____   DATE: _____

Work In Progress Report

Report Date:

Date:	Job No.	Name	Contract Amt	Paid to Date	Balance	Labor	Material/Cost	Job Cost	Profitability
Total:									

(Date)

Company
Address
City, State, Zip
Attn: Accounts Payable

Re: Account Number _____

Dear _____:

    In reviewing our accounts receivable, I noticed that your account is _____ days past due. At this time you owe a total of $_____.

    I would like to take this opportunity to remind you that our terms call for payment within 30 days of receipt of our invoice. Accordingly, anything you can do to expedite your payment would be appreciated.

    If there is a problem with your account or if I can assist you with any questions, please call me as soon as possible. Otherwise, please accept our thanks for your prompt payment and for any payment mailed in the last few days.

Very truly yours,

Name
Title

Date

Company
Address
City, State, Zip
Attn: Accounts Payable

Re: Account Number _____

Dear _____ :

On (date) we wrote to you regarding the past due status of your account. To date, we have not received any correspondence or payment from you. At the present time, your account is in excess of (_____) days old and the balance is currently $._____ .

The terms of our engagement provide for the addition of delinquency charge of 1 ½% percent per month for the period since the account was 30 days past due. Because we value your business, we are reluctant to take such action, but instead are appealing to your sense of responsibility to pay your debts.

As we have previously indicated, if you feel this amount is in error or if you are experiencing a current cash flow difficulty, please contact us immediately so we can work out another arrangement.

If your payment has been mailed within he last few days, please accept our thanks.

Very truly yours,

Name
Title

Company
Address
City, State, Zip
Attn: (President)

Re: Account Number _____

Dear _____:

      _____ has asked me to contact you regarding your seriously past due account.

      You must certainly be aware that it is not good business practice to allow an account to become _____ days past due. Accordingly, it is fast approaching the point where we must react to your apparent unwillingness to pay. If you are experiencing financial difficulties or you disagree with the charges, we would appreciate notification to that effect.

      We have recently initiated an aggressive program for the collection of delinquent accounts. In order that I may avoid submitting your account to our collections committee for processing, please call me within the next five (5) days to explain the delay and arrange for the payment of your account.

      Thank you for your cooperation in this very important matter.

Very truly yours,

Name
Title

EMPLOYEE NON-COMPETE AGREEMENT

In consideration of my being employed by _____
(Company), I, the undersigned, hereby agree that upon the termination of my employment
and notwithstanding the cause of termination, I shall not compete with the business of the
Company or its successors or assigns, to wit: _____ and
shall not directly or indirectly, as an owner, officer, director, employee, consultant, or
stockholder, engage in the business of _____ or a business
substantially similar or competitive to the business of the Company.

This non-compete agreement shall extend only for a radius of _____ miles from the present
location of the Company, and shall be in full force and effect for _____ years,
commencing with the date of the employment termination.

Singed and sealed this _____ day of _____, 20_____.

_____
Employee

_____   _____
Employer   Title

Example Sales Letter

name and address, attn:

date

Dear (Company, contact)

Save hundreds per month on your Business Bookkeeping!

Did you know that an independent bookkeeper can save you hundreds of dollars per month on Payroll Taxes, Workers Compensation and productive time lost?

Hiring even a part-time bookkeeper and placing them on your payroll is not always the most cost saving way of getting your books done. I would like the opportunity to show you how I can save you time and money doing your business bookkeeping.

Whether you are using QuickBooks®, Peachtree, or need to be set-up computerized to streamline your business finances, my experience and expertise in helping small businesses organize their books is a great asset to any company.

Call me today and I will include two free hours of on-site bookkeeping to get you on your way.

You can reach me at 555-555-1111 or 555-555-1112 and I would be happy to schedule a time to meet with you.

Yours sincerely

(Name)

Example Sales Letter

name and address, attn:

date

Dear (Company, contact)

Congratulations on your new business!

Now that you have your business up and running, have you considered how to proceed with your companies bookkeeping needs?

Don't fall into the 3-5 year category of businesses failing because you weren't prepared to handle your bookkeeping or taxes. We can set-up your computerized bookkeeping or utilize Write-Up Services. We also work diligently with Payroll Services, CPA's and other professionals to help you with all of your business needs.

Call me today and I will include two free hours of on-site bookkeeping to get you on your way.

You can reach me at 555-555-1111 or 555-555-1112 and I would be happy to schedule a time to meet with you.

Don't wait too long! Tax time likes to sneak up before you know it!

Yours sincerely

(Name)

Chapter 8

Additional Resources

QuickBooks Pro® Software is a registered trademark of Intuit®

Intuit: 1-888-246-8848

Turbo Tax®: 1-800-757-3279

Turbo Tax State®: 1-800-925-6720

www.quickbooks.com

www.intuit.com

www.quicken.com

www.turbotax.com

QuickBooks® Pro Advisor Program: www.quickbooks.com/press-partners/advisors/

Peachtree®

Best Software SB, Inc.

1505 Pavilion Place

Norcross, GA 30093   770-724-4000   www.peachtree.com

Peachtree Advisor: www.peachtree.com/forms/html/psclist.cfm

www.bestaccountantsnetwork.com

www.peachtree.com/download/trial.cfm

Internal Revenue Service   www.irs.gov

General Information: 1-800-829-1040

Forms and Publications: 1-800-829-3676

Tele-Tax Topics: 1-800-829-4477

You can download forms and publications online using Adobe Reader, the IRS has a link to download the free software from Adobe) located at: www.adobe.com

H&R Block   1-800-TAX-7733

Tax course   approximately $345.00   www.handrblock.com

American Institute of Professional Bookkeepers

Phone: 1-800-622-0121   www.aipb.org

Email: info@aipb.org

Quill Office Supplies   www.quill.com

Printing Companies:

      www.vistaprint.com

      www.onlineprinthouse.com

Web-Hosting and advertising Companies:

      www.adpro.com

      www.fuzzywebmaster.com

      www.27stars.com

      www.freewebsubmission.com

      www.bizland.com

The Internet is the best resource for obtaining forms and information. If you need to obtain IRS or State Forms, their website has all of the PDF versions of forms you could possibly think of.

SARAH EDWARDS ONLINE MARKETING COURSE

Course Description: Attracting Clients and Customers Develop Your Business, Independent Career or Professional Practice ... Even if You Hate to Sell because you deserve to support yourself doing what you most enjoy doing. Whether you are just now going out on your own or have already created your own career and want to increase your income, build a self-sustaining income for yourself in this 12-week course based on the with weekly personal coaching.

Learn How to:
- Discover Marketing Activities You Enjoy Doing and Do Well
- Create the Visibility You Need to Get Clients Coming to You
- Build Your Clientele from Referrals and Word of Mouth
- Develop Consensual Relationships with Potential Clients Built So They Welcome Instead of Resist and Reject Your Message
- Define a Specialty and Expertise that Draws Clients to You Based on Your Passions, Life Purpose and Mission
- Identify What Makes Your Talents, Products or Services Unique
- Choose from 65 Successful Marketing Activities and Learn the Secrets to How They Get Results
- Describe What You Offer in a Memorable Way without Hype
- Develop a Marketing Plan that Suits You, Your Time, Your Money and Your Life

You can cut out the coupon below to get the 10% discount on the Marketing Course.

A link to Pine Mountain is also available on www.inhomebookkeeping.bizland.com/links.htm

Reference: San Diego Business Accounting Solutions

Save 10%
Online Marketing Course "Attracting Clients & Customers"
Pine Mountain Institute

http://www.simplegoodlife.com/mywebPM/online_course_getbiz.htm

San Diego Business Accounting Solutions does not endorse nor confirm the contents of Universal Accountings product or instruction. Based upon privately received student reviews, their Accounting instruction is of a very good quality.

UNIVERSAL ACCOUNTING BOOKKEEPING AND ACCOUNTING COURSE

Paychex Locations

ALABAMA

BIRMINGHAM
3595 Grandview Parkway
Suite 200
Birmingham, AL 35243
(205) 970-6850
FAX: (205) 970-6550

ALASKA

Please contact our National Sales Department at 1-800-322-7292 for payroll processing in this state.

ARIZONA

PHOENIX
5353 N. 16th St.
Suite 200
Phoenix, AZ 85016
(602) 266-3660
FAX: (602) 279-0334

TUCSON
4400 E. Broadway
Suite 108
Tucson, AZ 85711
(520) 795-9771
FAX: (520) 795-3633

ARKANSAS

LITTLE ROCK
Plaza West
415 N. McKinley
Suite 270
Little Rock, AR 72205
(501) 558-3050
FAX: (501) 558-3070

CALIFORNIA

EAST BAY
3875 Hopyard Road
Suite 160
Pleasanton, CA 94588
(925) 416-8100
FAX: (925) 416-8140

BAKERSFIELD
5330 Office Center Court
Suite 65
Bakersfield, CA 93309
(661) 633-0807
FAX: (661) 633-0812

FRESNO
7355 N. Palm Ave.
Suite 100
Fresno, CA 93711
(559) 432-1100
FAX: (559) 438-2133

CENTRAL COAST/MONTEREY
180 Westridge Drive
Suite 100
Watsonville, CA 95076
(831) 722-9788
FAX: (831) 768-4964

INLAND EMPIRE
625 E. Carnegie Drive
Suite 150
San Bernardino, CA 92408
(909) 890-4660
FAX: (909) 890-4655

NORTH BAY
88 Rowland Way
Suite 100
Novato, CA 94945
(415) 899-0203
FAX: (415) 899-9793

LOS ANGELES
300 Corporate Pointe
Suite 150
Culver City, CA 90230
(310) 338-7900
FAX: (310) 338-7960

PALM SPRINGS
74-040 Highway 111
Suite JJ-4
Palm Desert, CA 92260
(760) 773-1082
FAX: (760) 773-1062

ORANGE COUNTY
200 E. Sandpointe
Suite 100

SAN LUIS OBISPO
1350 Marsh St.
San Luis Obispo, CA 93401

Santa Ana, CA 92707
(714) 438-4000
FAX: (714) 540-0327

PASADENA
251 S. Lake Ave.
Suite 200
Pasadena, CA 91101
(626) 440-8852
FAX: (626) 304-9299

SACRAMENTO
12150 Tributary Point Drive
Suite 200
Gold River, CA 95670
(916) 608-1400
FAX: (916) 608-1435

SAN FRANCISCO
1100 Grundy Lane
Suite 350
San Bruno, CA 94066
(650) 624-0777
FAX: (650) 589-6265

VENTURA
5280 Valentine Road
Suite 120
Ventura, CA 93003-7338
(805) 650-0611
FAX: (805) 650-3616

COLORADO

DENVER
4400 Kittredge St.
Suite 50
Denver, CO 80239
(303) 307-0505
FAX: (303) 307-8640

CONNECTICUT

HARTFORD
55 Capital Blvd.
Suite 302
Rocky Hill, CT 06067
(860) 257-0677
FAX: (860) 529-4048

DELAWARE

Please contact our National Sales Department at 1-800-322-7292 for payroll processing in this state.

DISTRICT OF COLUMBIA

WASHINGTON, D.C.
3060 Williams Drive
Fairfax, VA 22031
(703) 698-6910
FAX: (703) 207-9549

FLORIDA

Branch Offices

FORT MYERS
12621 World Plaza Lane

(805) 781-0253
FAX: (805) 781-0255

WOODLAND HILLS
6345 Balboa Blvd.
Building 1, Suite 208
Encino, CA 91316
(818) 654-9130
FAX: (818) 654-9133

SAN DIEGO
8520 Tech Way
Suite 200
San Diego, CA 92123
(858) 467-7000
FAX: (858) 569-0639

SAN JOSÉ
25 Metro Drive
Suite 210
San Jose, CA 95110
(408) 436-5530
FAX: (408) 436-0724

COLORADO SPRINGS
1155 Kelly Johnson Blvd.
Suite 111
Colorado Springs, CO 80920
(719) 531-6980
FAX: (719) 590-6033

STAMFORD
11 Riverbend Drive S.
P.O. Box 4816
Stamford, CT 06907-0816
(203) 973-1050
FAX: (203) 973-1070

SILVER SPRING
8300 Colesville Road
Suite 100A
Silver Spring, MD 20910
(301) 587-4748
FAX: (301) 587-2421

Sales Offices

SARASOTA
677 N. Washington Blvd.

Building #55
Fort Myers, FL 33907
(239) 277-7144
FAX: (239) 277-1832

JACKSONVILLE
8875 Liberty Ridge Drive
Suite 200
Jacksonville, FL 32256
(904) 363-3000
FAX: (904) 363-3143

ORLANDO
1001 Heathrow Park Lane
Suite 2001
Lake Mary, FL 32746
(407) 333-1338
FAX: (407) 333-2281

TAMPA
10105 Dr. Martin Luther
King Jr. St. N.
St. Petersburg, FL 33716
(727) 579-4700
FAX: (727) 579-4224

Sarasota, FL 34236
(877) 447-7217
FAX: (941) 952-5858

MIAMI
2801 S.W. 149th Ave.
Suite 110
Miramar, FL 33027
(954) 443-0442
FAX: (954) 430-1259

PALM BEACH
250 Australian Ave. S.
Suite 200
W. Palm Beach, FL 33401
(561) 655-5542
FAX: (561) 655-8960

GEORGIA

ATLANTA
600 Townpark Lane
Suite 100
Kennesaw, GA 30144
(678) 354-7776
FAX: (678) 354-0575

ATLANTA NORTH
2970 Clairmont Rd.
Suite 940
Atlanta, GA 30329
(678) 354-7776
FAX: (404) 471-1980

HAWAII

Please contact our National Sales Department at 1-800-322-7292 for payroll processing in this state.

IDAHO

Please contact our National Sales Department at 1-800-322-7292 for payroll processing in this state.

ILLINOIS

CHICAGO
4300 Weaver Parkway
Suite 100
Warrenville, IL 60555
(630) 848-1400
FAX: (630) 836-1900

CHICAGO, EAST
8505 W. 183rd St.
Suite C
Tinley Park, IL 60477
(708) 532-7725
FAX: (708) 614-1372

CHICAGO, DOWNTOWN
150 S. Wacker Drive
Suite 700
Chicago, IL 60606
(630) 848-1400
FAX: (312) 899-0859

CHICAGO, NORTH
191 Waukegan Rd.
Suite 202
Northfield, IL 60093
(630) 848-2778
FAX: (847) 446-5483

INDIANA

INDIANAPOLIS
9393 Delegate's Row
Indianapolis, IN 46240
(317) 815-9300
FAX: (317) 815-9902

SOUTH BEND
105 E. Jefferson Blvd.
Suite 800
South Bend, IN 46601
(574) 237-0939
FAX: (574) 280-2025

IOWA

Please contact our National Sales Department at 1-800-322-7292 for payroll processing in this state.

KANSAS

KANSAS CITY
13160 Foster St.
Suite 130
Overland Park, KS 66213
(913) 814-7776
FAX: (913) 814-9809

KENTUCKY

LEXINGTON
771 Corporate Drive
Suite 110
Lexington, KY 40503
(859) 224-3001
FAX: (859) 224-3023

LOUISVILLE
13400 Eastpoint Centre Drive
Suite 145
Louisville, KY 40223
(502) 245-6660
FAX: (502) 245-1084

LOUISIANA

NEW ORLEANS
Oakwood Corporate Center
401 Whitney Ave.
Suite 200
Gretna, LA 70056
(504) 368-4455
FAX: (504) 362-2884

BATON ROUGE
2900 Westfork Drive
Suite 200
Baton Rouge, LA 70827
(225) 298-1360
FAX: (225) 298-1361

MAINE

PORTLAND
6 Ashley Drive
Suite 100
Scarborough, ME 04074
(207) 883-2000
FAX: (207) 883-5942

MARYLAND

BALTIMORE
100 Painters Mill Road
Suite 300
Owings Mills, MD 21117
(410) 581-7700
FAX: (410) 581-7770

SILVER SPRING
8300 Colesville Road
Suite 100A
Silver Spring, MD 20910
(301) 587-4748
FAX: (301) 587-2421

MASSACHUSETTS

BOSTON
120 Presidential Way
Woburn, MA 01801
(781) 935-4500
FAX: (781) 935-6312

WORCESTER
Midstate Office Park
27A Midstate Drive
Suite 200
Auburn, MA 01501
(508) 832-0452
FAX: (508) 832-8379

MICHIGAN

DETROIT
29065 Cabot Drive
Novi, MI 48377
(248) 488-1100
FAX: (248) 994-7135

GRAND RAPIDS
625 Kenmoor Ave.
Suite 100
Grand Rapids, MI 49546
(616) 940-8855
FAX: (616) 940-8195

MINNESOTA

MINNEAPOLIS
(MMS available)
1210 Northland Drive
Suite 100
Mendota Heights, MN 55120
(651) 365-5060
FAX: (651) 365-5080

MISSISSIPPI

Please contact our National Sales Department at 1-800-322-7292 for payroll processing in this state.

MISSOURI

ST. LOUIS
16305 Swingley Ridge Road
Suite 500
Chesterfield, MO 63017
(636) 519-0340
FAX: (636) 537-5520

MONTANA

Please contact our National Sales Department at 1-800-322-7292 for payroll processing in this state.

NEBRASKA

OMAHA
(MMS available)
11128 John Galt Blvd.
Suite 25
Omaha, NE 68137
(402) 331-6600
FAX: (402) 339-2353

NEVADA

LAS VEGAS
(MMS available)
2340 Corporate Circle
Suite 175
Henderson, NV 89074
(702) 933-6200
FAX: (702) 933-6226

RENO
(MMS available)
1 E. Liberty St.
Suite 5
Sierra Executive Suites
Reno, NV 89504
(775) 686-6005
FAX: (775) 686-6043

NEW HAMPSHIRE

PORTSMOUTH
500 Spaulding Turnpike
Suite N-120
PO Box 3094
Portsmouth, NH 03801
(603) 433-1822
FAX: (603) 433-1810

MANCHESTER
43 Constitution Drive
Bedford, NH 03110
(603) 471-2590
FAX: (603) 471-1960

NEW JERSEY

CENTRAL NEW JERSEY
1551 S. Washington Ave.
Suite 200
Piscataway, NJ 08854
(732) 424-9394
FAX: (732) 424-9391

CHERRY HILL
30 Lake Center Executive Park
Suite 110
401 Route 73 N.
Marlton, NJ 08053
(856) 396-0100
FAX: (856) 396-0790

WOODCLIFF LAKE
135 Chestnut Ridge Road
2nd floor
Montvale, NJ 07645
(201) 930-0500
FAX: (201) 930-8812

NEW MEXICO

ALBUQUERQUE
8500 Menaul Blvd. N.E.
Suite A110
Albuquerque, NM 87112
(505) 293-3322
FAX: (505) 293-0666

NEW YORK

ALBANY
1365 Washington Ave.
Suite 201
Albany, NY 12206
(518) 435-9100
FAX: (518) 435-9188

BINGHAMTON
20 Hawley St.
4th Floor, East Tower
Binghamton, NY 13901
(607) 771-0965
FAX: (607) 724-2938

BUFFALO
33 Dodge Road
Suite 110
Getzville, NY 14068
(716) 688-0025
FAX: (716) 688-7419

BROOKLYN
45 Main St.
Suite 603
Brooklyn, NY 11201
(718) 222-9929
FAX: (718) 222-3910

LONG ISLAND
1393 Veterans Memorial Hwy.
Suite 110-N
Hauppauge, NY 11788
(631) 360-2700
FAX: (631) 360-7849

LAKE SUCCESS
3000 Marcus Ave.
Suite 1W6
Lake Success, NY 11042
(516) 437-1100
FAX: (516) 437-1033

MANHATTAN
1551 S. Washington Ave.
Suite 200
Piscataway, NJ 08854
(732) 968-2700
FAX: (732) 968-4879

MANHATTAN
1250 Broadway
Suite 2900
New York, NY 10001
(212) 239-9400
FAX: (212) 239-9494

MID HUDSON VALLEY
300 Westage Business Center
Route 9
Suite 150
Fishkill, NY 12524
(845) 896-6100
FAX: (845) 896-0468

ROCHESTER
105 Despatch Drive
E. Rochester, NY
14445-0509
(585) 218-5100
FAX: (585) 264-8555

SYRACUSE
990 James St.
Syracuse, NY 13203
(315) 474-1605
FAX: (315) 471-5831

NORTH CAROLINA

CHARLOTTE
9300 Harris Corners Parkway
Suite 150
Charlotte, NC 28269
(704) 599-0989
FAX: (704) 921-0776

GREENSBORO
4015 Meeting Way
Suite 101
High Point, NC 27265
(336) 841-5600
FAX: (336) 841-6004

RALEIGH
15501 Weston Parkway
Suite 100
Cary, NC 27513
(919) 678-9001
FAX: (919) 677-9823

WILMINGTON
Barclay Commons
2516 Independence Blvd.
Suite 106
Wilmington, NC 28412
(910) 798-7785
FAX: (910) 798-7790

NORTH DAKOTA

Please contact our National Sales Department at 1-800-322-7292 for payroll processing in this state.

OHIO

AKRON
3515 Massillon Road
Suite 150
Uniontown, OH 44685
(330) 896-6060
FAX: (330) 896-6080

CINCINNATI
Pfeiffer Place
10300 Alliance Road
Suite 500
Cincinnati, OH 45242
(513) 793-7800
FAX: (513) 936-6915

CLEVELAND
4760 Richmond Road
Suite 100
Warrensville Heights, OH 44128
(216) 292-1800
FAX: (216) 292-5922

COLUMBUS
5450 Frantz Road
Suite 100
Dublin, OH 43016
(614) 210-0400
FAX: (614) 734-9862

DAYTON
2 Prestige Place
Suite 160
Miamisburg, OH 45342
(937) 434-6311

TOLEDO
7010 Spring Meadows Drive W.
Suite 102
Holland, OH 43528
(419) 861-3388
FAX: (419) 861-3040

OKLAHOMA

OKLAHOMA CITY
(MMS available)
3525 N.W. 56th St.
Suite D-110
Oklahoma City, OK 73112
(405) 947-8869
FAX: (405) 948-6018

TULSA
9810 E. 42nd St.
Suite 100
Tulsa, OK 74146
(918) 663-2221
FAX: (918) 622-5958

OREGON

PORTLAND
7650 S.W. Beveland St.
Suite 100
Tigard, OR 97223
(503) 620-6800
FAX: (503) 639-7550

EUGENE
1142 Willagillespie Road
Suite 27
Eugene, OR 97401
(541) 484-4584
FAX: (541) 484-4791

PENNSYLVANIA

ALLENTOWN
7450 Tilghman St.
Suite 107
Allentown, PA 18106
(610) 398-7518
FAX: (610) 398-8632

SCRANTON/
WILKES-BARRE
1065 Highway 315
Suite C
Wilkes-Barre, PA 18702
(570) 822-5535
FAX: (570) 822-6476

HARRISBURG
500 Nationwide Drive
Suite 200

PHILADELPHIA
Valley Forge Corporate Center
1100 Adams Ave.

Harrisburg, PA 17110
(717) 526-4000
FAX: (717) 526-4020

PITTSBURGH
Foster Plaza IX
750 Holiday Drive
Pittsburgh, PA 15220
(412) 921-5090
FAX: (412) 921-5165

RHODE ISLAND

PROVIDENCE
501 Wampanoag Trail
E. Providence, RI 02915
(401) 435-3399
FAX: (401) 431-0923

SOUTH CAROLINA

GREENVILLE
430 Roper Mountain Rd.
Suite H-2
Greenville, SC 29615
(864) 213-4240
FAX: (864) 213-4245

SOUTH DAKOTA

Please contact our National Sales Department at 1-800-322-7292 for payroll processing in this state.

TENNESSEE

CHATTANOOGA
1200 Premier Drive
Suite 120
Chattanooga, TN 37421
(423) 296-2840
FAX: (423) 296-2852

NASHVILLE
22 Century Blvd.
Suite 150
Nashville, TN 37214
(615) 574-4343
FAX: (615) 883-8508

Norristown, PA 19403
(610) 650-8100
FAX: (610) 676-8350

MEMPHIS
6555 Quince Road
Suite 100
Memphis, TN 38119
(901) 753-2291
FAX: (901) 753-2491

TEXAS

DALLAS/FORT WORTH
6440 N. Beltline Road
Suite 100
Irving, TX 75063
(972) 518-0888
FAX: (972) 518-8059

HOUSTON
11777 Katy Freeway
Suite 200
Houston, TX 77079
(281) 588-1500
FAX: (281) 588-1554

AUSTIN
3636 Executive Center Drive
Suite G-52
Austin, TX 78731
(512) 469-0550
FAX: (512) 345-8345

FORT WORTH
3116 W. Fifth St.
Suite 107
Fort Worth, TX 76107
(817) 332-2061
FAX: (817) 336-2819

SAN ANTONIO
4242 Woodcock Drive
Suite 100
San Antonio, TX 78228
(210) 737-3700
FAX: (210) 733-1453

UTAH

SALT LAKE CITY
6955 Union Park Center
Suite 260
Midvale, UT 84047
(801) 561-3473
FAX: (801) 561-3644

VERMONT

Please contact our National Sales Department at 1-800-322-7292 for payroll processing in this state.

VIRGINIA

RICHMOND
3960 Stillman Parkway
Suite 100
Glen Allen, VA 23060
(804) 418-6600
FAX: (804) 418-6625

TIDEWATER
5700 Cleveland St.
Suite 120
Virginia Beach, VA 23462
(757) 490-8840
FAX: (757) 490-8736

WASHINGTON

SEATTLE
500 Naches Ave. S.W.
Suite 201
Renton, WA 98055
(425) 235-1112
FAX: (425) 235-5122

WEST VIRGINIA

Please contact our National Sales Department at 1-800-322-7292 for payroll processing in this state.

WISCONSIN

MILWAUKEE
(MMS available)
Corporate Woods Office
375 Bishops Way
Brookfield, WI 53005-6200
(262) 782-8123
FAX: (262) 782-9381

APPLETON
4650 W. Spencer St.
Suite 20
Appleton, WI 54914
(920) 733-5565
FAX: (920) 733-3182

MADISON
8413 Excelsior Drive
Suite 140
Madison, WI 53717
(608) 827-3100
FAX: (608) 829-1933

WYOMING

Please contact our National Sales Department at 1-800-322-7292 for payroll processing in this state

ADVANTAGE OFFICE LOCATIONS

ALABAMA
Birmingham
205-870-0605

CALIFORNIA
Oakland
925-416-2197
Orange County
714-730-4102
San Diego
858-467-7944

CONNECTICUT
Fairfield County
203-270-9670

GEORGIA
Atlanta
678-581-2447

ILLINOIS
Warrenville
630-836-1183

INDIANA
Evansville
812-485-2400

LOUISIANA
Baton Rouge
225-926-5640

MAINE
Auburn
207-784-0178
Bangor
207-945-0152
Presque Isle
207-764-6038

MASSACHUSETTS
Boston
978-369-4700
Concord
978-318-9990

MICHIGAN
Detroit
313-331-0500

MINNESOTA
Minneapolis
800-834-8393

NEW HAMPSHIRE
Manchester
800-244-1468

NEW YORK
Long Island
800-440-9033

PENNSYLVANIA
Ft. Washington
215-653-0850

RHODE ISLAND
Warwick
401-941-5600

SOUTH CAROLINA
Rock Hill
803-324-1190

TEXAS
Lubbock
806-785-9911
Midland
432-687-3304

WEST VIRGINIA
Wheeling
304-242-8787

ADP OFFICE LOCATOR

National Account Services Headquarters
5800 Windward Parkway
Alpharetta, Georgia 30005
(770) 360-2000

CALIFORNIA

CERRITOS SALES OFFICE
CERRITOS TOWNE CENTER
12610 PARK PLAZA DRIVE
CERRITOS, CA 90701
562-924-4999

CERRITOS WEST NATL SVC CTR
CERRITOS TOWNE CENTER
12610 PARK PLAZA DRIVE
CERRITOS, CA 90701
562-924-4999

SAN FRANCISCO SALES OFFICE
4125 HOPYARD ROAD
PLEASANTON, CA 94588
925-251-5300

SAN RAMON WEST SERVICE CENTER
4125 HOPYARD ROAD
PLEASANTON, CA 94588
925-251-5300

CONNECTICUT

MILFORD SALES OFFICE
CORPORATE CAMPUS II
612 WHEELERS FARMS ROAD
MILFORD, CT 06460-1600
203-876-5800

STAMFORD BENEFIT SERVICES
RIVERBEND CENTER
TWO OMEGA DRIVE
STAMFORD, CT 06907
203-355-2000

FLORIDA

JACKSONVILLE TIME & LABOR
MANAGEMENT
7014 A. C. SKINNER PARKWAY
SUITE 260
JACKSONVILLE, FL 32256
904-279-0040

MIAMI SALES OFFICE
7007 NORTHWEST 77TH AVENUE
MIAMI, FL 33166
305-882-7300

ORLANDO SALES OFFICE
5728 MAJOR BOULEVARD SUITE 100
ORLANDO, FL 32819
407-352-8282

TAMPA SALES OFFICE
4900 LEMON STREET
TAMPA FL 33609
(813) 287-6600

GEORGIA

NATIONAL ACCOUNT SERVICES-
DIVISION HQ
5800 WINDWARD PARKWAY
ALPHARETTA, GA 30005
770-360-2000

ATLANTA BENEFIT SERVICES
5800 WINDWARD PARKWAY
ALPHARETTA, GA 30005
770-360-2000

SOUTHERN REGION
ONE PREMIER PLAZA
5605 GLENRIDGE DRIVE, SUITE 670
ATLANTA, GA 30342
404-851-9910

ATLANTA COBRA BENEFIT SERVICES
2575 WESTSIDE PARKWAY
SUITE 500
ALPHARETTA, GA 30004
770-619-7200

ILLINOIS

DEERFIELD BENEFIT SERVICES
1419 LAKE COOK ROAD
DEERFIELD, IL 60015
847-267-3500
DEERFIELD RETIREMENT SERVICES
1419 LAKE COOK ROAD
DEERFIELD, IL 60015-3500
847-267-3500

CHICAGO SALES OFFICE
100 NORTHWEST POINT BOULEVARD
ELK GROVE VILLAGE, IL 60007
847-718-2000

CHICAGO MIDWEST NATL SVC CTR
100 NORTHWEST POINT BOULEVARD
ELK GROVE VILLAGE, IL 60007
847-718-2000

CENTRAL REGION
6400 SHAFER COURT, SUITE 740
ROSEMONT, IL 60018
847-318-0620

IOWA

DES MOINES BENEFIT SERVICES
1776 WEST LAKES PARKWAY
WEST DES MOINES, IA 50398
515-280-8100

KANSAS

KANSAS CITY SALES OFFICE
9705 LOIRET BLVD.
LENEXA, KS 66219
913-492-4200

KENTUCKY

LOUISVILLE RETIREMENT SERVICES
462 S. FOURTH AVENUE
900 MEIDINGER TOWER
LOUISVILLE, KY 40202-3431
502-561-8900

MARYLAND

CHESAPEAKE NORTH SALES OFFICE
11411 RED RUN BOULEVARD
OWINGS MILLS, MD 21117
800-575-2503

BALTIMORE SOUTHEAST SVC CENTER
11411 RED RUN BOULEVARD
OWINGS MILLS, MD 21117
800-660-4089

CHESAPEAKE SOUTH SALES OFFICE
2301 RESEARCH BOULEVARD
ROCKVILLE, MD 20850
800-829-5352

SILVER SPRING BENEFIT SERVICES
8403 COLESVILLE ROAD
METRO PLAZA 2, 13TH FLOOR
SILVER SPRING, MD 20910
301-562-3600

MASSACHUSETTS

BOSTON NEW ENGLAND NATL SVC CTR
225 SECOND AVENUE
WALTHAM, MA 02154-9081
781-890-2500

BOSTON SALES OFFICE
225 SECOND AVENUE
WALTHAM, MA 02454-9081
781-890-2500

MICHIGAN

ANN ARBOR HRIZON ALLIANCE/IPP
175 JACKSON PLAZA
ANN ARBOR, MI 48106
734-769-6800

DETROIT SALES OFFICE
16901 MICHIGAN AVENUE
DEARBORN, MI 48126
313-845-6583

MINNESOTA

MINNEAPOLIS SALES OFFICE
8100 CEDAR AVENUE
BLOOMINGTON, MN 55425-1805
952-854-1700

NEW JERSEY

CLIFTON EAST NATL SVC CTR
205 MAIN AVENUE
CLIFTON, NJ 07014
973-365-7300

CLIFTON SALES OFFICE
205 MAIN AVENUE
CLIFTON, NJ 07014
973-365-7300

MORRESTOWN SALES OFFICE
2 EXECUTIVE DRIVE, #9
MORRESTOWN, NJ 08057
856-437-3030

EASTERN REGION
ONE GATEWAY CENTER, SUITE 103
NEWARK, NJ 07102
973-242-2300

ROSELAND RETIREMENT SERVICES
4 BECKER FARM ROAD
ROSELAND, NJ 07068-1728
973-994-5000

ROSELAND - TOTAL PAY
1 ADP BOULEVARD
ROSELAND NJ 07068
(973) 974-5000

NEW YORK

LONG ISLAND SALES OFFICE
1700 WALT WHITMAN ROAD
MELVILLE, NY 11746-3078
631-694-7800

MANHATTAN SALES OFFICE
1 PENN PLAZA, 23RD FLOOR
NEW YORK, NY 10119
212-563-2233

NORTH CAROLINA

CHARLOTTE SALES OFFICE
7400 CARMEL EXECUTIVE PARK, #310
CHARLOTTE, NC 28226
704-540-4160

OHIO

CINCINNATI SALES OFFICE
500 W. SEVENTH STREET
CINCINNATI, OH 45203-1594
513-852-5200

CLEVELAND SALES OFFICE
7007 E. PLEASANT VALLEY ROAD
INDEPENDENCE, OH 44131
216-447-1980

OREGON

PORTLAND WEST SERVICE CENTER
10155 SE SUNNYSIDE ROAD
CLACKAMAS, OR 97015
503-654-6800

PORTLAND SALES OFFICE
10155 SE SUNNYSIDE ROAD
CLACKAMAS, OR 97015
503-654-6800

TENNESSEE

NASHVILLE SALES OFFICE
810 ROYAL PARKWAY, SUITE 100
NASHVILLE, TN 37214
615-885-7470

TEXAS

DALLAS SALES OFFICE
1349 EMPIRE CENTRAL, #500
DALLAS, TX 75207-2211
214-905-2771

HOUSTON SALES OFFICE
13141 NORTHWEST FREEWAY
HOUSTON, TX 77040-6399
713-939-4600

UTAH

SALT LAKE CITY BENEFIT SERVICES
2835 S. DECKER LAKE DRIVE
SALT LAKE CITY, UT 84119
801-956-6000

WASHINGTON

SEATTLE RETIREMENT SERVICES
ONE UNION SQUARE SUITE 2812
600 UNIVERSITY AVENUE
SEATTLE, WA 98101-1184
206-292-2020

INDEX

Glossary

Accounting cycle – the series of accounting activities included in recording financial information for a fiscal period.

Accounting system – a planned process for providing financial information that will be useful to management.

Account number – the number assigned to an account.

Accounts payable ledger – a subsidiary ledger containing only accounts for vendors from whom items are purchased or bought on account.

Accounts receivable ledger – a subsidiary ledger containing only accounts for charge customers.

Account title – the name given to an account.

Accrued expenses – expenses incurred in one fiscal period but not paid until a later fiscal period.

Accrued interest expense – interest incurred but not yet paid.

Accrued interest income – interest earned but not yet received.

Accrued revenue – revenue earned in one fiscal period but not yet received until a later fiscal period.

Accumulated depreciation – the total amount of depreciation expense that has been recorded since the purchase of a plant asset.

Adjusting entries – journal entries recorded to update general ledger accounts at the end of a fiscal period.

Adjustments – changes recorded on a worksheet to update general ledger accounts at the end of a fiscal period.

Allowance method of recording losses from uncollectible accounts – crediting the estimated value of uncollectible accounts to a contra account.

Assessed value – the value of an asset determined by tax authorities for the purpose of calculating taxes.

Asset – anything of value that is owned.

Bad debts – see uncollectible accounts.

Balance sheet – a financial statement that reports assets, liabilities, and owner's equity on a specific date.

Bookkeeper – a person who does general accounting work plus some summarizing and analyzing of accounting information.

Calendar year – 12-month calendar starting January 1st and ending December 31st.

Capital – the account used to summarize the owner's equity in the business.

Capital stock – total shares of ownership in a corporation.

Cash over – a petty cash on hand amount that is more than a recorded amount.

Cash payments journal – a special journal used to record only cash receipt transactions.

Cash sale – a sale in which cash is received for the total amount of the sale at the time of the transaction.

Cash short – a petty cash on hand amount that is less than a recorded amount.

Chart of accounts – a list of accounts used by a business.

Closing entries – journal entries used to prepare temporary accounts for a new fiscal period.

Correcting entry – a journal entry made to correct an error in the ledger.

Cost of goods sold – the price a business pays for goods it purchases to sell.

Credit – an amount recorded on the right side of a T account.

Current assets – cash and other assets expected to be exchanged for cash or consumed within a year.

Current liabilities – liabilities due within a short time, usually within a year.

Customer – a person or business to whom merchandise or services are sold.

Debit – an amount recorded on the left side of a T account.

Declining-balance method of depreciation – multiplying the book value at the end of each fiscal period by a constant depreciation rate.

Depreciation expense – the portion of a plant asset's cost that is transferred to an expense account in each fiscal period during a plant asset's useful life.

Distribution of net income statement – a partnership financial statement showing distribution of net income or net loss to partners.

Dividends – earnings distributed to stockholders.

Double-entry accounting – the recording of debit and credit parts of a transaction.

Employee earnings record – a business form used to record details affecting payments made to an employee.

Entry – information for each transaction recorded in a journal.

Equities – financial rights to the assets of a business.

Expense – a decrease in owner's equity resulting from the operation of a business.

Federal unemployment tax – a federal tax used for state and federal administrative expenses of the unemployment program.

FICA tax – a federal tax paid by employees and employers for old-age, survivors, disability, and hospitalization insurance.

Fiscal period – the length of time for which a business summarizes and reports financial information.

Fiscal year – 12-month accounting period.

General journal – a journal with two amount columns in which all kinds of entries can be recorded.

General ledger – a ledger that contains all accounts needed to prepare financial statements.

Gross profit on sales – the revenue remaining after cost of merchandise (goods) sold has been deducted.

Income statement – a financial statement showing the revenue and expenses for a fiscal period.

Interest expense – the interest accrued on money borrowed.

Interest income – the interest earned on money loaned.

Inventory – the amount of goods on hand.

Liability – an amount owed by a business.

Long-term liabilities – liabilities owed for more than one year.

Manual accounting – an accounting system in which data are recorded and reported mostly by hand.

Medicare – the federal health insurance program for people who have reached retirement age.

Net income – the difference between total revenue and total expenses when total revenue is greater.

Net loss – the difference between total revenue and total expenses when total expenses is greater.

Net earnings – the total earnings paid to an employee after payroll taxes and other deductions.

Notes payable – promissory notes that a business issues to creditor.

Notes receivable – promissory notes that a business accepts from customers.

Owner's equity – the amount remaining after the value of all liabilities is subtracted from the value of all assets.

Owner's equity statement – a financial statement that summarizes the changes in owner's equity during a fiscal period.

Partner – each member of a partnership.

Partnership – a business in which two or more persons combine their assets and skills.

Pay period – the period covered by a salary payment.

Payroll – the total amount earned by all employees for a pay period.

Payroll register – a business form used to record payroll information.

Payroll taxes – taxes based on the payroll of a business.

Post-closing trial balance – a trial balance prepared after the closing entries are posted.

Posting – transferring information from a journal entry to a ledger account.

Proprietorship – a business owned by one person.

Ratio – a comparison between two numbers showing how many times one number exceeds the other.

Real property – land and anything attached to the land.

Retained earnings – an amount earned by a corporation and not yet distributed to stockholders.

Revenue – an increase in owner's equity resulting from the operation of a business.

Reversing entry – an entry made at the beginning of one fiscal period to reverse an adjusting entry made in the previous fiscal period.

Salary – the money paid for employee service.

Sales Tax – a tax on a sale of merchandise or services.

Schedule of accounts payable – a listing of vendor accounts, account balances, and total amount due all vendors.

Schedule of accounts receivable – a listing of customer accounts, account balances, and total amount due from all customers.

Service business – a business that performs an activity for a fee.

Share of stock – each unit of ownership in a corporation.

Social Security tax – see FICA.
Sole proprietor – see proprietorship.

State unemployment tax – a state tax used to pay benefits to unemployed workers.

Statement of stockholders' equity – a financial statement that shows changes in a corporation's ownership for a fiscal period.

Stockholder – an owner of one or more shares of a corporation.

Straight-line method of depreciation – charging an equal amount of depreciation expense for a plant asset in each year of its useful life.
Sum – the answer to an addition problem.

Supporting schedule – a report prepared to give details about an item on a principal financial statement.
T-account – an accounting device used to analyze transactions.

Tax base – the maximum amount of earnings on which a tax is calculated.

Temporary accounts – accounts used to accumulate information until it is transferred to the owner's capital account.

Total earnings – the total pay due for a pay period before deductions (**gross pay).**

Transaction – a business activity that changes assets, liabilities, or owner's equity.

Trial Balance – a proof of the equality of debits and credits in a general ledger.

Un-collectible accounts – accounts receivable that cannot be collected.

Vendor – a business from which merchandise is purchased or supplies or other assets are bought.

Working capital – the amount of total current assets less total current liabilities.

Work sheet – a columnar accounting form used to summarize the general ledger information needed to prepare financial statements.

Writing off an account – canceling the balance of a customer account because the customer does not pay.

Rock Castle Construction
Account Listing

Account	Type
1100 · Checking	Bank
1101 · Savings	Bank
1105 · Petty Cash	Bank
1110 · Accounts Receivable	Accounts Receivable
1120 · Inventory Asset	Other Current Asset
1121 · Employee Loans	Other Current Asset
1125 · Prepaid Expenses	Other Current Asset
1125 · Prepaid Expenses:1125.01 · Legal Retainer	Other Current Asset
1125 · Prepaid Expenses:1125.02 · Insurance	Other Current Asset
1130 · Undeposited funds	Other Current Asset
1140 · Organizational Costs	Other Current Asset
1141 · Accumulated Amortization	Other Current Asset
1150 · Fixed Asset	Fixed Asset
1150 · Fixed Asset:1150.01 · Office Furniture & Equipment	Fixed Asset
1150 · Fixed Asset:1150.02 · Vehicles	Fixed Asset
1150 · Fixed Asset:1150.03 · Tools & Equipment	Fixed Asset
1150 · Fixed Asset:1150.04 · Accumulated Depreciation	Fixed Asset
1175 · Accounts Payables	Accounts Payable
1200 · Credit Card	Credit Card
1200 · Credit Card:1200.01 · Visa	Credit Card
1200 · Credit Card:1200.02 · CalOil Card	Credit Card
1225 · Capital Loan Payable	Other Current Liability
1225 · Capital Loan Payable:1225.01 · Owner 1	Other Current Liability
1225 · Capital Loan Payable:1225.02 · Owner 2	Other Current Liability
1250 · Payroll Liabilities	Other Current Liability
1250 · Payroll Liabilities:Company	Other Current Liability
1250 · Payroll Liabilities:Company:Fica	Other Current Liability
1250 · Payroll Liabilities:Company:Medicare	Other Current Liability
1250 · Payroll Liabilities:Company:Futa	Other Current Liability
1250 · Payroll Liabilities:Company:Suta	Other Current Liability
1250 · Payroll Liabilities:Employee	Other Current Liability
1250 · Payroll Liabilities:Employee:Federal Withholding	Other Current Liability
1250 · Payroll Liabilities:Employee:State Withholding	Other Current Liability
1250 · Payroll Liabilities:Employee:Fica	Other Current Liability
1250 · Payroll Liabilities:Employee:Medicare	Other Current Liability
1250 · Payroll Liabilities:Employee:SDI	Other Current Liability
1280 · Sales Tax Payable	Other Current Liability
1285 · Notes Payable	Other Current Liability
1285 · Notes Payable:1285.01 · Truck Loan	Other Current Liability
1285 · Notes Payable:1285.02 · Other Notes	Other Current Liability
1300 · Opening Bal Equity	Equity
1304 · Owner's Capital	Equity
1304 · Owner's Capital:1304.01 · Owners Contribution	Equity
1304 · Owner's Capital:1304.02 · Owner's Draw	Equity
1305 · Retained Earnings	Equity

Rock Castle Construction
Account Listing

Account	Type
1350 · Construction	Income
1350 · Construction:1350.01 · Room Additions	Income
1350 · Construction:1350.02 · Intererior Remodling	Income
1350 · Construction:1350.03 · Exterior Structures	Income
1350 · Construction:1350.04 · Miscellaneous	Income
1350 · Construction:1350.05 · Discounts Given	Income
1375 · Cost of Goods Sold	Cost of Goods Sold
1375 · Cost of Goods Sold:1375.01 · Job Expenses	Cost of Goods Sold
1375 · Cost of Goods Sold:1375.02 · Job Materials	Cost of Goods Sold
1375 · Cost of Goods Sold:1375.03 · Permits and Licenses	Cost of Goods Sold
1375 · Cost of Goods Sold:1375.04 · Subcontractors	Cost of Goods Sold
1375 · Cost of Goods Sold:1375.05 · Tools and Machinery	Cost of Goods Sold
1375 · Cost of Goods Sold:1375.06 · Equipment Rental	Cost of Goods Sold
1400 · Advertising Expense	Expense
1402 · Automobile Expense	Expense
1402 · Automobile Expense:1402.03 · Inusrance	Expense
1402 · Automobile Expense:1402.01 · Repairs & Maintenance	Expense
1402 · Automobile Expense:1402.02 · Fuel	Expense
1403 · Bank Service Charges	Expense
1404 · Bad Debt	Expense
1406 · Amortization	Expense
1407 · Depreciation Expense	Expense
1408 · Dues and Subscriptions	Expense
1408 · Dues and Subscriptions:1408.01 · Union Dues	Expense
1410 · License and Permits	Expense
1411 · Interest Expense	Expense
1411 · Interest Expense:1411.01 · Finance Charges	Expense
1411 · Interest Expense:1411.02 · Loan Interest	Expense
1415 · Miscellaneous	Expense
1417 · Insurance	Expense
1417 · Insurance:1417.01 · Disability Insurance	Expense
1417 · Insurance:1417.02 · Liability Insurance	Expense
1417 · Insurance:1417.03 · Workers Compensation	Expense
1425 · Office Expense	Expense
1430 · Office Supplies	Expense
1440 · Payroll Expenses	Expense
1440 · Payroll Expenses:1440.01 · Administration Salaries	Expense
1440 · Payroll Expenses:1440.02 · Labor	Expense
1440 · Payroll Expenses:1440.03 · Bonuses	Expense
1440 · Payroll Expenses:1440.04 · Fees	Expense
1440 · Payroll Expenses:1440.05 · Taxes	Expense
1440 · Payroll Expenses:1440.05 · Taxes:Company Medicare	Expense
1440 · Payroll Expenses:1440.05 · Taxes:Company Fica	Expense
1440 · Payroll Expenses:1440.05 · Taxes:Futa	Expense
1440 · Payroll Expenses:1440.05 · Taxes:Suta	Expense
1450 · Postage and Delivery	Expense

Rock Castle Construction
Account Listing

Account	Type
1452 · Printing and Reproduction	Expense
1455 · Professional Fees	Expense
1455 · Professional Fees:1455.01 · Accounting	Expense
1455 · Professional Fees:1455.02 · Legal Fees	Expense
1460 · Rent	Expense
1470 · Repairs	Expense
1470 · Repairs:1470.01 · Building Repairs	Expense
1470 · Repairs:1470.02 · Computer Repairs	Expense
1470 · Repairs:1470.03 · Equipment Repairs	Expense
1475 · Taxes	Expense
1475 · Taxes:1475.01 · Federal	Expense
1475 · Taxes:1475.02 · State	Expense
1475 · Taxes:1475.03 · Property	Expense
1475 · Taxes:1475.04 · Local	Expense
1480 · Telephone	Expense
1495 · Utilities	Expense
1495 · Utilities:1495.01 · Gas and Electric	Expense
1495 · Utilities:1495.02 · Water	Expense
1500 · Void Check Listing	Expense
1550 · Other Income	Other Income
1550 · Other Income:1550.01 · Interest Income	Other Income
1560 · Other Expenses	Other Expense

NOTES

NOTES

NOTES

NOTES

NOTES

NOTES